THE ORIGIN

OF THE

Canon of the Old Testament.

An Historico-Critical Enquiry

BY

Dr. G. WILDEBOER,
Professor at Groningen.

TRANSLATED BY
BENJAMIN WISNER BACON, *M. A., D. D.*
EDITED WITH PREFACE BY PROF. GEORGE F. MOORE.

WIPF & STOCK · Eugene, Oregon

Wipf and Stock Publishers
199 W 8th Ave, Suite 3
Eugene, OR 97401

The Origin of the Canon of the Old Testament
An Historico-Critical Enquiry
By Wildeboer, G. and Bacon, Benjamin W.
ISBN 13: 978-1-62564-713-9
Publication date 3/13/2014
Previously published by Luzac & Co., 1895

$Μεγάλη\ ἡ\ ἀλήθεια\ καὶ\ ὑπερισχύει.$
1 **Esdras** 4, 41.

AUTHOR'S PREFACE TO THE FIRST EDITION.

In publishing this investigation of the origin of the Canon of the Old Testament the author hopes in some measure to supply a lack. Of course, a great deal has been written about the Canon, as may be seen from the literature at the end of Strack's article, "Kanon" in Herzog's Real-Encyclopaedie [*2 ed. VII. p. 45 f.*], *and every work on Introduction has something on the subject. To name only the best of much that is good, I refer to the close of the third part of Prof. Kuenen's* Historisch-Kritisch Onderzoek naar het Ontstaan en de Verzameling van de Boeken des Ouden Verbonds, *Leiden, 1865, III. p. 394—450. What is there given is almost absolutely complete, and it is needless to say that all the material has been subjected to most thorough criticism.*

I have felt constrained, however, to offer something additional and something of a different kind. Something additional; because, naturally, a quarter of a century after Kuenen's excellent work, there is somewhat more to be said. But my purpose was, also, to publish a work of somewhat different character. I do not refer here to more or less considerable differences of opinion, but to the different plan of the work. I have tried to arrive at a tenable conception of the history of canonization, and have given particular attention to the causes and motives which were operative in it.* *Much which was out of place in an Introduction may be properly discussed here. To this fact paragraphs such as the eighth, on the Idea of Canonicity in the Jewish Schools, and the twelfth, owe their existence. I have also introduced some additional material, and, in particular, have treated with some fulness the evidence afforded by the New Testament. But in this respect the book may speak for itself.*

It seemed to me desirable that a volume of moderate size should be published on the origin of the Canon of the Old Testament. I hope that it may prove to be a plain guide for students in their studies, and one that, at the same time, stimulates them to go further into the history of the origin of the books of the Bible. How closely both the external and the internal history of the Canon is connected with this, will be apparent at every step.

I hope that my book may come also into the hands of such as have already left the University. Many of them cannot spare the time to follow the isagogic studies about the Pentateuch and the other books of the Old Testament. But it is certainly possible to study a book

---

* I need not say — for reasons which will be obvious in the following pages — that I entirely disagree with Geiger, when he writes (*Nachgelassene Schriften*, 1876, IV. p. 17): "So ist die ganze weit ausgesponnene Untersuchung über den Kanon und die kritische Resultate, die man daran knüpfte, ein Schaumgebilde." I believe that the historical evidence, properly examined, enables us to form an idea of the history which in the main satisfies the demands of science.

like this of scarcely a hundred and fifty pages. And a good insight into the way in which the books of the Old Testament were brought together is a solid basis for a sound idea of the Bible.

I am aware that this volume contains many truths which are unwelcome to many even among Theologians. What do I expect of them? Let me not answer this question, but rather say what I hope from them. I hope that they will seriously examine such views as I present, and if they think it their duty to do so, will controvert them with solid arguments.

Finally, whatever may be done, I still steadfastly believe with the author of 3 (1) Esdras the words which he makes Zerubbabel address to King Darius (3, 12): "Truth is victorious over all." And the word of the people (4, 41), which has passed into a proverb, remains true: "Great is truth, and exceeding powerful."

GRONINGEN, May 11, 1889.   G. WILDEBOER.

PREFACE TO THE SECOND EDITION.

When, in Autumn of *1889*, my investigation of the Origin of the Canon of the Old Testament appeared, I thought that by the publication of it a lack would be supplied. I hoped that my work would be appreciated by students of theology, and that some ministers also might take note of it.

This hope has not been disappointed; indeed, the result has far surpassed my expectation. In our own country and beyond our borders, the book has been kindly received and favorably criticised. It sold so rapidly that within a year the publisher began to talk of a second impression; and now after less than a year and a half, I send out this second edition.

For this edition I have gratefully made use of the observations and animadversions of my various critics. In part I could not but recognize the justice of these criticisms, and to them my work is indebted for many improvements. In part they gave me occasion to express myself more clearly or to give my reasons more explicitly. For this, too, notwithstanding our difference of opinion, I am under obligations to them.

I have been able also to take note of the latest work

on this subject, by Professor Frants Buhl, Kanon und Text des Alten Testaments, *Leipzig, 1891. On many points he expresses his agreement with me; on some he is of a different opinion. His arguments have not convinced me, for reasons which I have given in their place. Various additions and corrections, of greater or less magnitude, which upon reperusal appeared to me necessary, have been embodied in this second edition.*

What is now offered to the theological public may thus properly be called a revised and enlarged edition.

With gratitude and confidence I commend my work to the attention of all who are interested in Old Testament investigation.

GRONINGEN, Jan. 3, 1891.   G. WILDEBOER.

EDITOR'S PREFACE.

Professor Wildeboer's Historico-Critical Enquiry into the Origin of the Old Testament Canon has deservedly received high commendation from scholars of different countries and various schools. Since its first publication in 1889 it has passed through a second edition in the original (1891) and has been translated into German (Gotha: Perthes, 1891); and the wish has been frequently expressed that it might be made accessible to English students also. When it first came out there was no other work of the kind which satisfactorily represented the present state of Old Testament learning. Buhl's excellent little book, Den Gammeltestamentlige Skriftoverlevering, &c. (Kopenhagen, 1885), *seems hardly to have been known outside the limits of his own country. Since that time have appeared Professor Buhl's* Kanon und Text des Alten Testaments *(Leipzig, 1891), and Professor Ryle's* Canon of the Old Testament *(London & New York, 1892). The former has also been translated into English, by the Rev. John Macpherson;* Canon and Text of the Old Testament *(Edinburgh, 1892). The scope and plan of these works are, however, so different from those of the present volume that they do not render a translation* *of it superfluous. Professor Wildeboer has rightly entitled his work An Historico-Critical Enquiry, rather than a History of the Old Testament Canon: the method of investigation is followed throughout, both in the arrangement of the book and the presentation of the material. It is therefore peculiarly adapted to the use of students of theology, clergymen, and others who wish to examine the evidence on this important question for themselves. This method has, in the present state of Old Testament criticism, another very great merit: it separates the question of the collection and canonization of the sacred books from that of their origin and age, and thus makes it as far as possible independent of the results of the so-called higher criticism, which in a descriptive history of the Canon like Ryle's are necessarily assumed at the outset. The two lines of investigation thus become mutually corroborative or corrective.* In the confidence that the work will be found to meet the needs of English students as well as it has proved to do in Holland and Germany this translation is presented to them.*

The translation, from the second edition of the original with numerous additions and corrections by the author, has been made by the Rev. B. W. Bacon, of Oswego, N. Y., whose own contributions to the criticism of

---

* Professor Wildeboer has since published *De Letterkunde des Ouden Verbonds naar de tijdsorde van haar ontstaan*, Groningen, 1893, an Introduction to the Old Testament Literature, in chronological order, in which his views upon questions of Old Testament criticism will be found fully stated. It has been translated into German: *Die Litt. des A. T.* u. s. w. Göttingen, Van den Hoeck und Ruprecht, 1895.

the Old Testament have earned him a good name among scholars.

In editing the volume, particular care has been given to the quotations and references, especially in the field of Jewish literature, where the inevitable aberration of translation at second hand has been corrected by recourse to the original. References to English translations of Dutch and German books have been given, where such exist; and a few more recent titles have been added. Notes and references for which the editor is responsible, whether in the text or foot notes, are enclosed in brackets.

GEORGE F. MOORE.

ANDOVER, Mass., August 14, 1894.

CONTENTS.

	PAGE.
Introduction...............................	1.
§ 1. The Parts of the Old Testament Canon..........	5.
§ 2. The Threefold Division of the Old Testament. Preliminary Inferences........................	15.
§ 3. Historical Evidence concerning the Canon of the Old Testament.	
a. In the Old Testament.....................	22.
§ 4. Historical Evidence concerning the Canon of the Old Testament, continued.	
b. In Jewish Greek Literature................	30.
§ 5. Historical Evidence concerning the Canon of the Old Testament, continued.	
c. In the New Testament....................	47.
§ 6. Historical Evidence concerning the Canon of the Old Testament, continued.	
d. In Palestinian Jewish Sources, especially in the Talmud................................	56.
§ 7. Historical Evidence concerning the Canon of the Old Testament, continued.	
e. The Christian Church Fathers	75.
§ 8. The Idea of Canonicity in the Jewish Schools.....	86.

		PAGE.
§ 9.	History of the Collection of the Old Testament Books.	
	a. The Canonization of the Law	101.
§ 10.	History of the Collection of the Old Testament Books, continued.	
	b. The Canonization of the Prophets	114.
§ 11.	History of the Collection of the Old Testament Books, continued.	
	c. The Canonization of the "Writings" and close of the Canon of the Old Testament	136.
§ 12.	Conclusion...................................	153.
	Index of Names and Subjects...........	167.
	Index of passages from Bible, Talmud &c..	174.
	Errata.......................................	181.

INTRODUCTION.

A thorough investigation of the history of the collection of the books of the Old Testament and of the significance which must consequently be attached to the term "canonical" as used in the Jewish synagogue is of the highest importance to Christian theologians, and by no means superfluous.

It is not superfluous; for the Christian church has constantly followed, more or less closely, in the leading-strings of Jewish scholars, and Protestant theologians especially have conceived that in so doing they were taking the safest course [1].

Such an investigation is also of the highest importance. For a clear insight into the way in which the books of the Old Testament acquired their canonical authority in the synagogue enables us justly to estimate the standard employed by the scribes, and thus to liberate ourselves from the Jewish tradition, which at bottom is directly opposite to the Christian view of the Old Testament [2].

[1] It may seem strange that no œcumenical council of the early church decided the question what books of the Old Testament were to be regarded among Christians as canonical. While the church as a whole, after sore conflicts, gave its judgment in regard to the Trinity, Christology and Soteriology, it formulated no doctrine concerning the Canon or Inspiration. The first œcumenical council which made a deliverance about the canonicity of the books of the Old Testament was the council of Trent (1546); but this was no longer a general assembly of all Christendom.

In the Oriental church, especially after the labours of Origen, there was a disposition to follow the Jewish schools. In the West the influence of Jerome was supplanted by Augustine. The habitual following of the *consuetudo ecclesiæ* gradually brought the West to perceive that the Christian church possessed a different Canon from the synagogue (see Diestel, *Geschichte des Alten Testaments in der Christlichen Kirche*, 1869, p. 69 ff.).

With the Reformation came a change. Its principle, the return to Holy Scripture, involved the enquiry as to the original Bible. In this investigation the Protestants surrendered themselves to the guidance of the Jewish scholars of their time. In this way Jewish tradition gained the ascendency, as it was expounded by Elias Levita in the third Preface of his widely-read treatise *Masoreth hammasoreth* (completed in 1538)[*], and as it appears to have been accepted by most of the Jewish

---

[*] [C. D. Ginsburg, *The Massoreth ha-massoreth of Elias Levita in Hebrew with an English translation*, &c., London, 1867].

scholars of the Middle Ages, — at least Rabbi David Kimchi
(† 1240) appears already inclined to this view. (Herzog's *Real
Encyclopædie*, 2 ed., art. "*Kanon,*" VII. p. 416).

Since the Christian church has thus adopted more or less
completely the tradition of the Jews it is advisable to inspect
this tradition closely, and to bring it to the test of well established
historical facts. Our investigation subserves this end.

2 It will appear in the course of our investigation that the
standard applied by the Jewish scribes is such as would never
have been employed by Christian theologians. How it came
that a standard in our eyes so false has done no more harm,
so that in the main the Christian church had no reason
to diverge on this point from the synagogue, will appear plainly
hereafter. The preliminary remark may, however, be made, that
the whole view of the Jewish theologians about the Law and
its absolutely unique significance by no means corresponds to
what the Christian church, taught by the Apostle Paul, has
learned to see in the O. T.

The history of the collection of the Old Testament
books may very justly be regarded as a continuation of the history of the origin of these books.
Our investigation frequently presupposes assured
results of historical criticism concerning the origin
of the Old Testament writings. Yet our enquiry
as a whole is not based upon these results; and
the arguments which we borrow from the results
of historical criticism concerning the origin of these
books are so elucidated and corroborated from an

other side that they do not much affect the certainty of our conclusions one way or the other [3]. There is therefore no objection to treating separately the enquiry into the history of canonization of the Old Testament books.

[3] Thus e. g. we shall deduce from the late date of the book of Daniel, at least in its present form (about 165 B.C.), more than one inference concerning the canonization of the second collection, and draw from the late date of Chronicles (about 250 B.C.) an argument regarding the canonization of the third collection. But it will appear that our determination of the date of the canonization of the second collection is based upon other grounds, and that the fact that Daniel finds its place in the third collection is itself evidence of its late date. The same is the case with Chronicles.

The literature of our subject may be found in Herzog's *P. R. E.*[2], art. "Kanon des A. T.", VII. p. 450 ff (H. L. Strack). To this may be added: H. Graetz, *Kohélet, oder der Salomonische Prediger*, Leipzig 1871; Anhang I, "Der alttestamentliche Kanon und sein Abschluss," p. 147—173; J. S. Bloch, *Studien zur Geschichte der Sammlung der Althebräischen Literatur*, Breslau, 1876; F. Buhl, *Kanon und Text des Alten Testaments*, Leipzig 1891; H. E. Ryle, *The Canon of the Old Testament*, London 1892. Especially to be commended is W. Robertson Smith, *The Old Testament in the Jewish Church*, 2 ed., Edinburgh, 1892, Lecture VI., p. 149—187. For the history of post-exilic Judaism consult E. Schürer, *Geschichte des Jüdischen Volkes im Zeitalter Jesu Christi*, Leipzig, 1886—1890, 2 vols.; English translation, *History of the Jewish People in the time of Jesus Christ.*, Edinburg & New-York, 1891, 5 vols.; H. Oort, *De Laatste Eeuwen van*

Israël's Volksbestaan, 's Gravenhage 1877; O. Holtzmann, *Das Ende des Jüdischen Staatswesen und die Entstehung des Christenthums;* in Stade and Holtzmann's, *Gesch. des Volkes Israel,* II. 2.; P. Hay Hunter, *After the Exile; a hundred years of Jewish history and literature*, 1890, 2 vols.

§ 1.

THE PARTS OF THE OLD TESTAMENT CANON.

There exists no specific name for the books of the Old Testament as a whole. In ancient times very general terms were employed, such as "the Scripture,"[1] or the whole was called "the Law" in conformity with the fundamental character of the Tora[2]. Later, figurative appellations[3] and a technical term[4] came into use. The Christian name "Old Testament" has come into established use from the Vulgate translation of 2 Cor. 3, 14[5].

---

[1] The sacred Scriptures are often called מִקְרָא (Neh. 8, 8), especially in contrast to Mishna and Talmud. Also "The Twenty Four" *sc.* Books. Further כִּתְבֵי הַקֹּדֶשׁ, הַכָּתוּב, &c. In the N. T. ἡ γραφή, αἱ γραφαί.

[2] It is not without significance, as will appear hereafter, that the entire O. T. is cited as תורה (*Sanhedrin*, 91*b*);

also in the N. T. as ὁ νόμος, Joh. 10, 34. 12, 34. 15, 25. 1 Cor. 14, 21.

3 As a figurative term we must mention the name מקדשיה (*mikdashya*, sanctuary of Yawhé), which appears in the subscription of a Bible manuscript as early as the year 1486 (*P. R. E.*[2], *VII. p.* 439).

4 In the Massora the name תנך occurs very frequently as an abbreviation for the names of the three divisions of the O. T.: כתובים, נביאים, תורה.

5 Ἡ παλαιὰ διαθήκη is there incorrectly rendered by Old Testament. Διαθήκη is the translation of the Hebrew ברית; it is better therefore to translate διαθήκη by *covenant*, except in Heb. 9, 15—17 and perhaps Gal. 3, 17. True, the LXX translators, whose usage is followed by the N. T. writers, did not go altogether amiss in giving διαθήκη the preference over συνθήκη as a rendering of ברית, in order thereby to indicate that in the Hebrew word the idea of reciprocity is not prominent, but that the covenant is an ordinance of God. But if we choose to hold here to the Alexandrian exegetical tradition we should render διαθήκη by *statutum*, and in Heb. 9, 15—17, and perhaps in Gal. 3, 17, think simply of statutum *ultimum*. In Latin Christendom διαθήκη was very early rendered by *testamentum*; but Tertullian opposed the custom and endeavored to bring into use a different translation, *instrumentum*. This attempt was not wholly fruitless, but the less accurate popular rendering at last carried the day and received definitive sanction through the Vulgate. It is singular that Tertullian himself retained the popular word in the translation of the Bible. On this point see further, Th. Zahn, *Geschichte des Neutestamentlichen Kanons*, Erlangen, 1888, I. p. 105 ff.

§ 1. THE PARTS OF THE OLD TESTAMENT CANON.

The Old Testament consists of three parts, תורה, נביאים, and כתובים. The Tora is divided into חֲמִשָּׁה חוּמְשֵׁי הַתּוֹרָה, the five fifths of the law. Each of the five books derives its Hebrew name from its initial word or words, while our appellations are borrowed either from the Greek version of the LXX. through the Vulgate (Genesis, Exodus, Deuteronomy) or from the Vulgate alone (Leviticus, Numbers)[6]. The Nebiim are divided into 1. נביאים ראשונים, prophetae priores (Joshua, Judges, Samuel, Kings), and 2. נביאים אחרונים, prophetae posteriores. The latter were further distinguished as (*a*) נביאים גדולים (Isaiah, Jeremiah, Ezekiel), and (*b*) נביאים קטנים, which, as appears from the fact that Malachi alone is followed by a subscription, together form a single book, שנים עשר or in Aramaic תְּרֵיסַר or תרי עשר, τὸ δωδεκαπρόφητον[7]. The Kethubim consist of (*a*) the books אמ״ת (Psalms, Proverbs, Job),* (*b*) the חמש מגלות, the five rolls (Canticles, Ruth, Lamentations, Ecclesiastes, Esther), (*c*) Daniel, Ezra, Nehemiah and Chronicles[8].

---

[6] For public reading in the synagogue the Tora is divided in manuscripts (from which the division has passed over into

* Better תא״ם, according to which *vox memorialis* Job would come before Proverbs. See Delitzsch, *Commentar über die Psalmen*, 4 ed. 1883, p. 3, n. 2. [*Commentary on the Psalms*, London: Hodder & Stoughton, 1887, I. p. 3 f.; Elias Levita, ed. Ginsburg, p. 248.]

our printed editions of the Massoretic text) into *parashas* (רשׁה, section). Of these there are three kinds. The smallest parashas [paragraphs], 379 in number, are indicated by a ס (i. e. סתומה or סמוכה, 'closed', *scil.*, line). A space of three letters was left blank before and after the ס, but the rest of the line might be filled out (closed). The larger parashas [paragraphs], 290 in number, are indicated by a פ (i. e. תוחה, 'open', *scil.*, line). Before and after the פ a space of nine letters was left blank and a new (open) line always begun. The largest parashas [pericopes], 54 in number are indicated by פפפ when they coincide with a פ and by ססס when they coincide with a ס, and in our editions are also designated by numerals running from 1 to 54. In 35 instances they coincide with a פ and are marked פפפ, and 13 times they coincide with a ס and are indicated by ססס; furthermore a new parasha begins with each book, and in Gen. 47, 28 the division coincides neither with ס nor with פ and is designated only by the numeral.

These rules were not always observed by the later copyists; whence it comes to pass that we do not always find in our printed editions a blank space of three letters before and after a ס or of nine letters before and after a פ. The division into 54 parashas is of Babylonian origin and designed to be read through in course in one year. It is of liturgical character, which is not the case with the division into 379 or 290 parashas; these more resemble the later division into chapters, and were originally employed in other O. T. books also. (Buhl, *Kanon*, p. 225 = Engl. trans., p. 223.) *. The first pericope is read on the Sabbath following the Feast of Tabernacles, and the last on the closing day of the next Feast of Tabernacles (23d of Tishri). This day is consequently

---

* [See Hupfeld, *Hebräische Grammatik*, 1841, § 19. Baer in his editions endeavors to restore these paragraphs; see Ginsburg, Preface to the 3d vol. of his *Massorah*].

§ 1. THE PARTS OF THE OLD TESTAMENT CANON.

called the Feast of Rejoicing for the Law (תורה שמחת), or Feast of the Tora. (Zunz, *Die gottesdienstlichen Vorträge der Juden*, Berlin 1832, p. 4; 2 ed., Frankfurt a. M., 1892, p. 4). This annual cycle was not universally adopted until the 14th century.

7 To correspond with the fifty four Sabbath lessons of the Law, fifty four lessons were selected from the Nebiim, which seemed to the Jewish scholars to be appropriate to the former respectively. These are called הפטרות. After the reading of a portion of the Tora in the synagogue it was the custom, certainly from as early a time as the age of the Maccabees* if not earlier, to close with the reading of a passage from the Prophets, הפטיר בנביא. Thus *e. g.* with the parasha "Bereshith" (Gen. 1, 1—6, 9) Is. 42, 5—43, 11 is read, and with the parasha "Noah" (Gen. 6, 9—11, 32) Is. 54, 1—10. In the time of Jesus it was customary in the synagogue to read from the Prophets also (Lu. 4, 16. 17; Acts. 13, 15. 17). The Law was then divided into 154 parashas, that it might be read through in course once in three years. With this agrees the division of the Pentateuch into 153 *Sedarim* in the Rabbinic Bibles**, or into 175 parashas according to the Jerusalem Talmud, in order to read the Law through in course of 3 or 3½ years. (Zunz, *Die Gottesdienstliche Vorträge*, u. s. w., p. 3, and Buhl, *Kanon*, p. 228 = Eng. trans. p. 225 f.) As regards the Prophets, it would seem that in the time of Jesus the reader himself selected a passage.

---

* [Zunz, *Gottesdienstl. Vorträge*, 2 ed. p. 5; but see König, *Einleitung in das Alte Testament*, 1893, p. 465.]

** [R. Jacob b. Hayim states that there are 154 *Sedarim*, but himself enumerates only 153. (Strack, *Prolegomena critica*, p. 77). See further on this division the authors cited by Harris, *Jewish Quarterly Review*, I. 1889, p. 227, n. 1; also Büchler *J. Qu. Rev.*, V. 420—465, 2 VI. 1—73].

Hence Luke 4, 16. 17 cannot be employed as a point of departure for a more exact chronology of the life of Jesus. The words ἐν Ἡλίᾳ in Rom. 11, 2 probably refer to no established haphtara, but point nevertheless to the antiquity of the practise of designating a passage by the name of the leading character or principal subject of the narrative. The same is perhaps the case with the words ἐπὶ Ἀβιάθαρ in Mark. 2, 26; while ἐπὶ τοῦ βάτου in Mark. 12, 26 may refer to one of the 154 or 175 parashas into which the Law was divided about the first century A. D.

⁸ Another division of the Kethubim is as follows: (a) שלשה גדולים כתובים, the three major writings, viz., the books א״מת, Ruth being inserted before the Psalms as an introduction, on account of the Davidic genealogy Ruth 4, 18—22; these were כתובים ראשונים: (b) כתובים קטנים, the minor writings, viz. Canticles, Ecclesiastes, and Lamentations: (c) כתובים אחרונים, the posterior writings, viz. the historico-prophetic writings of the third group, which included Esther, Daniel, Ezra-Nehemiah, and Chronicles. (See Fürst, *Der Kanon des A. T. nach den Ueberlieferungen in Talmud und Midrasch*, 1868, p. 60, 82, 100). The five Megilloth are thus not always put together, as in our editions, between the books א״מת and the last four books; in the classification just mentioned Esther is assigned to the last group and Ruth to the first. Three of the five Megilloth then remain as Kethubim Ketannim, while the first group is called Kethubim Rishonim and the third Kethubim Acharonim. Occasionally Ecclesiastes follows immediately after Proverbs and is numbered with the Kethubim Rishonim. (Cf. § 11, n. 14).

The statements regarding the number of the books as well as their order are conflicting. The oldest enumeration would seem to have been twenty four [9]. As regards the order, according to the Talmud Jeremiah precedes Ezekiel and Isaiah [10], while Ruth is the first book of the Kethubim and still other transpositions occur. The Massorites placed Isaiah first as the oldest, and are followed in this respect by German manuscripts as also by our editions. Another arrangement of the Massorites, making Chronicles the first instead of last book of the Kethubim and giving a different order of the five Megilloth, has been adopted in Spanish, but not in German manuscripts. Our printed editions, like the German manuscripts, have Chronicles as the last book and arrange the five Megilloth in the order in which they are read on various feasts and anniversaries [11]. It can scarcely be determined with certainty whether the Talmudic order is the original one; but there is no sufficient ground for the assumption that as late as three centuries after Christ Ruth and Lamentations were included by the Jews in the second division [12].

[9] The count of 24 books, which first appears in 4 (2) Esdras (toward the end of the first century A. D.), is universal in Talmud and Midrash; that of 22, obtained by connecting Ruth with Judges and Lamentations with Jeremiah, is of Alexandrian origin. The opinion of Schrader-de Wette (*Lehrbuch der histo-risch-kritischen Einleitung in die Bibel Alten und Neuen Tes-taments*, I. Berlin, 1869, § 10, p. 15) that the number 24 in these writings is based upon the number of letters in the Greek

alphabet, as 22 among the Alexandrians upon that of the Hebrew letters, is incorrect (*cf.* § 7 n. 2). The number 22 nowhere appears in Palestinian sources; though it may possibly be presupposed in the Book of Jubilees. (See Strack in *P. R. E²*., VII. p. 434—438). The number 35 in the late Midrash upon Numbers * is obtained by counting the Minor Prophets [excluding Jonah]. Our count of 39 books is derived from the LXX, in which, in addition to the separate enumeration of the Minor Prophets, Samuel, Kings, Chronicles, and Ezra-Nehemiah are each divided into two books, a subdivision which does not appear in the Talmud. This subdivision has through the Vulgate become universal in Christian editions and versions of the Bible. From the Vulgate it was introduced in the 16th century into the Hebrew Bible through the various editions of Daniel Bomberg in Venice, *e. g.* that of 1517—1518 [in folio, and 1518 in quarto], and especially through his Great Bible of 1525—26, edited by Rabbi Jacob ben Hayim which became the basis of all subsequent Hebrew Bibles.

The division into chapters is also of Christian origin, originating with Stephen Langton († 1228), later Archbishop of Canterbury, not with Hugo de Scto Caro († 1263), as is still commonly stated. See Schrader-de Wette, *Einleitung*, 1869, p. 164; cf. E. Nestle, *Lit. Centralblatt*, Feb. 13, 1892**. It is found in the first Bomberg editions (1518) and has since been universally introduced into the Hebrew Bible. It had even earlier been used by Jewish scholars for purposes of reference, not only by R. Nathan in his great concordance (about 1450; printed by Bomberg 1523), but—not long after its introduction in the Vulgate—by R. Shelomo ben Ishmael, as Dr. Schiller-Szinessy has pointed

---

* [See below § 6 n. 8.]

** [Schmid, *Ueber verschiedene Eintheilungen der heiligen Schrift*, u. s. w. 1892, p. 56 ff.; Moore, "The Vulgate Chapters and Numbered Verses in the Hebrew Bible;" *Journ. Bibl. Literature*, 1893, p. 73—78].

§ 1. THE PARTS OF THE OLD TESTAMENT CANON. 13

out. (See *The Prayer Book interleaved*, Cambridge 1877; *Theol. Tijdschrift*, 1878, p. 104.)

[10] The Talmudic order is as follows *Nebiim:* Jos. Jud. Sam. Kgs. Jer. Ez. Is. Twelve (minor) Prophets; *Kethubim:* Ruth, Psalms, Job, Prov. Eccl. Cant. Lam. Daniel, Esther, Ezra, and Chron. Why in the Talmud Jeremiah and Ezekiel precede the earlier Isaiah it is impossible to say with certainty. It may conceivably be because Jeremiah was regarded as the author of the Book of Kings, which immediately precedes It may also be that in this order is preserved a reminiscence of the fact that Isaiah as well as the Dodekapropheton is a collection of different prophecies. (Kuenen, *H. K. O¹.*, III. p. 449, n. 6; and G. A. Marx, *Traditio rabbinorum veterrima de librorum V. T. ordine atque origine*, Lipsiae, 1884, p. 13, f., 20 f; [2 (title) ed. under the name, G. Dalman, *Traditio rabbinorum, etc.* Lips. 1891]). In the Babylonian Gemara, *Baba Bathra* fol. 14^b—15^a we read: "The order of the prophetical books is, Joshua, Judges, Samuel, Kings, Jeremiah, Ezekiel, Isaiah, the Twelve. Inasmuch as Hosea was the first, as it is written, "The beginning of the word of the Lord by Hosea" (Hos. 1, 2) — [we should expect the book of Hosea to occupy the first place, at least of the four contemporary prophets, Hos. Is. Am. Mi.] But because his prophecy is written together with those of the latest prophets, Haggai, Zechariah, and Malachi, he is counted with them. Inasmuch as Isaiah was earlier than Jeremiah and Ezekiel the book of Isaiah ought to occupy the first place. But since the book of Kings ends with destruction and Jeremiah is all destruction, while Ezekiel begins with destruction and ends with consolation and Isaiah is all consolation, destruction was connected with destruction and consolation with consolation. The order of the Kethubim is: Ruth, and Psalms, and Job, and Proverbs, Ecclesiastes, Canticles, and Lamentations, Daniel and Esther, Ezra and Chronicles".*

---

* [See Marx, *op. cit.*].

14   § 1. THE PARTS OF THE OLD TESTAMENT CANON.

¹¹ Canticles, on account of the allegorical application to the deliverance out of Egypt, which appears in the Targum [on 1, 4], is read in the synagogue on the eighth day of the Passover; Ruth, the friendly harvest idyll, on the second day of Pentecost; Lamentations on the 9th of Ab (destruction of Jerusalem); Ecclesiastes on the third day of the Feast of Tabernacles, upon which it would seem to have been needful to remind men that the pleasures of life are only to be enjoyed with the eye upon God; and Esther at Purim. These are the only books of the Kethubim which are employed in the synagogue service. For this purpose they are written upon separate rolls, whence the name "The Five Rolls".

¹² The arrangement which makes Chronicles the last book of the Kethubim is probably the oldest, as we should perhaps infer from Matt. 23, 35 (cf. § 5, n. 3) as well as on account of the connection with Ezra and Nehemiah. Kuenen (*H. K. O*¹. III. p. 450 n. 8; see however *Theologisch Tijdschrift*, 1889, p. 645), thought that the present and Talmudic arrangement, which counts Ruth and Lam. among the Hagiographa, originated about 390 A. D., and that Jerome's testimony in his famous *Prologus galeatus* (cf. § 7 n. 3) indicates opposition to it. But the inclusion of Ruth and Lam. among the Nebiim is connected in Jerome with the enumeration of 22 books instead of 24. Of this enumeration, however, there is no certain trace either in the Talmud or the Midrash. Jerome's view is accordingly most probably to be explained by Alexandrian influence, which may very well have made itself felt in the Jewish circles from which Jerome drew his information. It should not be forgotten how easily such an order could be altered, since scarcely any one had a complete copy of all the books of the O. T., and hence the list of its books was for the majority a theory and nothing more. In the post-Talmudic tract *Sopherim* (iii. 6) permission is given to combine all the books in rolls of inferior importance,

but the synagogue rolls must contain all the books separately (cf. § 11, n. 2 and the foot note there; see further Joel Müller, *Masechet Soferim*, 1878, iii. 1 and iii. 5, and Marx, *Traditio rabbinorum vet.*, p. 28 f.).

§ 2.

THE THREEFOLD DIVISION OF THE OLD TESTAMENT CANON: PRELIMINARY INFERENCES.

Of the subjects introduced in the preceding paragraph, the threefold division of the Hebrew Old Testament must be taken up separately; for the reason that an attentive examination of this fact puts us at once in a position to draw preliminary inferences regarding the origin of the Canon.

This division cannot be the work of a single man nor of a single authoritative body. If this were the case we ought to be able to point out some manifest material difference between the different sections. For the Tora such a distinctive character can easily be shown; but no one has succeeded in satisfactorily defining the specific difference between the Nebiim and the Kethubim [1].

§ 2. THE THREEFOLD DIVISION OF THE O. T. CANON.

1 The threefold division of the O. T. canon itself conflicts with the traditional conception which ascribes the work of canonization to Ezra and the Men of the Great Synagogue (see § 6). The demand we have made is altogether fair, and, as appears from the attempts which have been made to solve the difficulty, is generally acknowledged to be fair. In order to maintain the tradition we must be able to point to some material difference between the several groups. The Tora is obviously distinguished by its legal character. The great mass of laws, particularly in the last three books, is evidence enough. The narrative in the first five books of the Bible is in large part either a preparation for the legislation, or a framework in which it is set; moreover many of the stories when carefully scrutinized are found to serve the purpose of emphasizing its injunctions or prohibitions. But no such sharply defined character can be ascribed to either the second or the third division as a whole.

The question therefore is, wherein do the Nebiim differ from the Kethubim? Various attempts have been made to show such a difference, but none of these can be said to be successful (cf. Kuenen *H. K. O*[1]., III. p. 444 ff.).

1⁰. Principally among Jewish theologians the attempt has been made to explain the difference between the second and third sections by the theory that the Prophets were inspired by the "spirit of prophecy", the Writings by "the holy spirit". The two groups were thus characterized by a different degree of inspiration. Moses Maimonides († 1204), who presents a developed doctrine of inspiration in which he distinguishes eleven degrees, applies this distinction also to the last two sections of the Canon. The Tora was revealed פֶּה אֶל פֶּה (Num. 12, 8); the Nebiim by the רוּחַ הַנְּבוּאָה and the Kethubim by the רוּחַ הַקֹּדֶשׁ. (*Moré Nebochim*, ii. 45; [= *Guide of the Perplexed*, transl. by M. Friedländer, vol. II (1885), p. 205 ff.]). Similarly David

Kimchi († 1240), in the Preface to his Commentary on the Psalms, and Abarbanel (born 1437) in the Preface to his Commentary on Joshua (a Latin translation in Joh. Buxtorfi fil. *Dissertationes philologico-theologicae*, Basel, 1657, p. 496—499).

This theory, which as may readily be imagined found little acceptance among Protestant theologians, must be imputed exclusively to these later Jewish scholars. Nowhere in the Old or New Testament, or even in the Talmud, is there any trace of this distinction. The "holy spirit" and the "spirit of prophecy" are identical. In the days of Ezra this mediaeval distinction was quite unknown.

2°. A second attempt is based upon a distinction made by Herm. Witsius, *Miscellanea sacra*, Lugd. Bat., 1736, I. p. 12. He distinguishes the *donum* from the *munus propheticum*. "Distingui ergo in prophetia potest, *Donum*, quod et privatis contigit, et in revelatione rerum arcanarum consistit, et *Munus*, quod extraordinaria in Ecclesia functio erat, certarum quarundam personarum, speciali vocatione Divina eo destinatarum." Hengstenberg (*Beiträge zur Einleitung in das Alte Testament*, 3 Bde., Berlin, 1831—1839, I. p. 23—30) bases upon this the theory that the compilers of the O. T. Canon incorporated into the second section the writings of those who possessed the *munus propheticum*, while in the third group were included the works of those who could boast only of the *donum propheticum*. The former were called, according to Hengstenberg, נביאים; the latter merely ראים and חזים (seers). Hengstenberg further added (having in mind the case of Daniel) the necessary restriction, that for a book to be included in the second section it was not sufficient that its author was a נביא; he must also have written in that character. (p. 28.)

This theory was further expounded by Hävernick (*Einleitung*, I. 1., 2 Aufl. 1854, p. 55 ff.) and adopted by Keil (*Handbuch der Einleitung in die Schriften des A. T.*, 3e Aufl. 1873, § 155).

Daniel was not a prophet. His book contains "die bedeutsame Lebensführung eines Nichtpropheten mit den ihm zu Theil gewordenen Offenbarungen".

Every one must see how far-fetched this whole argument is. There is indeed in the O. T. a prophetic order, and the scriptures contain oracles by one, at least, who was unwilling to bear the name נביא. But precisely this Amos (7, 12 ff.) overthrows the whole theory; for according to it his book ought to stand among the Kethubim. And is Daniel not a prophet? What then becomes of Matt. 24, 15? Moreover, there is a distinction between נביא and ראה; but what this distinction is, is taught much more correctly in 1 Sam. 9, 9. In our O. T. the terms are used promiscuously.

3°. Less forced is the attempt of G. F. Oehler (*Prolegomena zur Theologie des A. T.*, Stuttgart, 1845, p. 91 ff., and Art. "Kanon" in *P. R. E*¹., VII. p. 243 ff.). This scholar is of the opinion that the threefold division of the O. T. Canon corresponds to the development of the religion of Israel, the stages of which he thinks may be indicated by the names Mosaism, Prophetism, and Hebraism. The foundation is laid in the Law, its further development in an objective direction is found in the Prophets, in a subjective direction in the Writings. In other words, the classification of the O. T. books was made by the collectors according to the position of the authors in the economy of divine revelation.

This distinction holds good, in fact, of many parts of the Kethubim in contrast to parts of the Nebiim. There is a difference between the prophets, who announce the solemn testimony of Yahwé to his people, and the psalmists or authors of proverbs. But it again does not hold true of the two divisions as a whole. And this is precisely the question. Why, for example, is the priestly pragmatism of Ezra, Nehemiah and Chronicles more subjective than the prophetic pragmatism of Judges, Samuel and Kings?

No one of the attempted solutions can thus be regarded as successful. They all bear the mark of having been invented "pour le besoin de la cause." We are obliged, therefore, to seek a different explanation.

The examination of the three parts of the O. T. Canon has already shown us that the collection of these books cannot have been the work of a single man nor of a single body, because of the absence of any characteristic difference between the three divisions. This inference is further confirmed by the fact, that, following the example of the Greek translation of the LXX, none of the versions take any notice of the tripartite division. This can only be explained by the assumption that originally there was no well defined distinction between the second and third section [2].

[2] We refer to the fact that in the manuscripts of the LXX the historical books of the [Hebrew] third section follow in regular order upon those of the second. These manuscripts are indeed, at the earliest, of the 4th or 5th century after Christ, and of Christian origin; but Josephus (cf. § 4) confirms the antiquity of this order (*Contra Apionem* i, 8). Among those who were affected by Alexandrian influence Ruth also was connected with Judges and Lamentations with Jeremiah. In Alexandria their ideas about the Canon, were no doubt, less definite than in Palestine, but, in view of the active intercourse which was maintained between the Jewish colony in Alexandria and the mother-country and of the intellectual dependence of Alexandria upon Palestine,

it is highly improbable that they would have disregarded a well defined distinction between the two groups, sanctioned by an authoritative body. (See further § 11, n. 2.) From the LXX this arrangement of the books passed over into other versions, and has thus (through the Vulgate) become established in our English bibles also.

The testimony of Jerome (see § 1, n. 10 and § 7) should be estimated at its true value. Doubtless in his time the division was well established in authoritative Jewish circles; at least there is not the slightest evidence to the contrary in the Talmud or Midrash. Nevertheless the Alexandrian theory may have impressed Jerome's Jewish authorities as acceptable. (See further § 11, n. 2.)

An attentive examination accordingly, both of the Hebrew Old Testament and of the English versions and their predecessors, already throws some light upon the way in which the collection originated. Upon no single principle can the distinction between the second and third sections as wholes be explained. Only in part is a material difference between Nebiim and Kethubim to be recognized. What is not to be explained in this way puts us upon the conjecture that the difference must be chronological [3].

[3] It has become manifest to us that no general principle distinguishing the last two sections of the canon from each other can be discovered. We have seen, furthermore, that in ancient times no sharp distinction of the two sections was known. This

leads us to think that we have here to do with an historical process, and that the sequence of the three sections, so far as their canonical authority is concerned, is chronological. The collection of the last two groups may have been begun simultaneously, but the conjecture then lies close at hand that the second section was the first to be regarded as sacred, and that the third only attained this recognition after a considerable lapse of time. Daniel, Chronicles, Ezra, Nehemiah were then not incorporated in the second section, for the reason that it was regarded as complete.

The three divisions of the O. T. in their successive canonization represent the three principal epochs of post-exilic history: 1. from the end of the Babylonian captivity to Ezra; 2. from Ezra and Nehemiah to the Maccabees; 3. from the Maccabees to the end of Jewish history (cf. Ewald, *Geschichte des Volkes Israel*, 3e Aufl., 1864—1868, VII. p. 458—484 [= *History of Israel*, VIII. (1886) p. 312 ff.]).

But there is also an element of truth in what Oehler has maintained. There is in large degree a difference of contents. From the beginning on there probably existed, by the side of the Law, a collection of books having a double character, which formed the basis of the second and third sections. The Psalms, Proverbs and Job are plainly different from the Prophets, and this must have led, in the process of collection, to a division. Our further enquiry accordingly must thus take account of this twofold truth, that both a chronological and a material difference gave occasion to the distinction between Nebiim and Kethubim.

§ 3.

HISTORICAL EVIDENCE CONCERNING THE CANON OF THE OLD TESTAMENT.

a. IN THE OLD TESTAMENT.

Of an Old Testament Canon, even in the restricted sense of an authoritative collection of religious writings, there is no trace in the Old Testament before the Babylonian exile [1]. The laying up of laws or important documents "before Yahwé" has a different significance, as has likewise the collection of religious writings of which accounts have come down to us [2]. Only the solemn covenant concluded in the reign of Josiah on the basis of the law-book found in the temple (2 Kings 23, 2 ff.) can be regarded as the earliest, pre-exilic, beginning of the canonization of Old Testament scriptures [3].

[1] The sole place in the O. T. which can be appealed to in support of the opposite opinion is Is. 34, 16. Here the rendering of the R. V. is, "Seek ye out of the book of the LORD and read". Many interpreters, such as Knobel, Hitzig, Kuenen (*H. K. O.*[1], III. p. 399), connect the first word דרשו with the preceding verse and emend vs. 16 after the LXX, which gives a totally different reading. Verses 15 and 16 would then be read and translated thus: 15. "There the arrowsnake maketh her nest

and layeth her eggs, and hatcheth them, and gathereth her young in the shadow; yea, there do the vultures gather, each (vulture) seeketh her mate. 16. According to their number Yahwé calleth them up, none of them is missing, neither one nor the other is lacking; for his (Yahwé's) mouth hath commanded it, it is his breath that hath gathered them." But even apart from this, in our opinion necessary, emendation, and assuming that Is. 34 is a pre-exilic prophecy, this verse says nothing about a collection of Sacred Scriptures. The "book of Yahwé" is in the context nothing else than the body of the prophet's own oracles. The prophet appeals to posterity: He that survives the judgment upon Edom, let him only search in these sacred pages, and he will discover a striking coincidence between what is there foretold and what then comes to pass. (Delitzsch, *Commentar über das Buch Jesaia*, 4 ed., Leipzig, 1889, S. 363 [see also Dillm, Duhm, König, *Einleitung*, p. 439]).

² Various accounts of the depositing of the Decalogue and other laws of the Mosaic Tora, or of important documents, in the Jerusalem temple or some other sanctuary attract our attention (Ex. 40, 20; cf. 25, 22. 31, 18. 38, 21. Lev. 24, 3; Deut. 31, 9. 26. Jos. 24, 25; cf. 1 Sam. 10, 25). According to the attitude which is taken to the problem of the origin of the Hexateuch, judgments will differ about these passages, and investigators are not agreed about the meaning and extent of "the book of the law of God" (Jos. 24, 26). However, the passages cited say no more for the supporters of tradition than for us. The credibility of these accounts is left out of consideration. The fact that there is mention on more than one occasion of the laying up of laws and the like in temples is sufficient proof that the thing was done (cf. Cheyne, *Jeremiah, his life and times*, London, 1889, p. 84, 85). But the question for our purpose is what this laying up signified. On this point Keil, an unimpeachable witness, has

observed that it is inadmissible to draw from this the conclusion that there existed a pre-exilic collection of scriptures. He rightly compares it with the practice of other peoples. This preservation of laws in the sanctuaries was not for the purpose of forming a collection, but as a witness, in order that Yahwé might interpose with punishment when this law was transgressed (Keil, *Einleitung in das A. T.*, 3 ed. 1873, § 153 [= *Introduction*, 1870, § 153]). Compare also 2 Kings 11, 12, where Jehoiada the high priest at the coronation of Joash places a crown upon the head of the King and "the testimony" (הָעֵדוּת). This may be a transcriptional error for הָאֶצְעָדוֹת, "the bracelets" (see 2 Sam. 1, 10), as Wellhausen (Bleek's *Einleitung in das A. T.*, 4 Aufl., Berlin, 1878, p. 258, n. 1. [not repeated in *Composition des Hexateuchs*, u. s. w. 1889, p. 294]) conjectures. But even if the Massoretic reading, which also appears in the LXX, be retained, this passage only proves that at the solemn coronation of a prince, among other things a roll of the law, such as were preserved for the purpose above mentioned in the temple, was held above his head as a symbol that above the king stood Yahwé's will, which he was called to maintain.

That poetical productions were collected, for instance by "Hezekiah's men" (Prov. 25, 1), or still earlier in the *Sepher Hayyashar* and the *Sepher Milchamoth Yahwé* (Jos. 10, 13. Num. 21, 14) and that teaching them to the people was enjoined (Deut. 31, 19. 2 Sam. 1, 18) can hardly be adduced as proof that a Canon existed before the exile.

In Ps. 40, 8, finally, reference is made to "a book roll", מְגִלַּת סֵפֶר. The rendering of vs. 8 is doubtful; see the various commentaries. Perhaps the last four words were originally a marginal gloss to explain vs. 9*a* (see Dyserinck, *de Psalmen uit het Hebreeuwsch op nieuw vertaald, &c.* Haarlem, 1877, p. 60, n. 7). But whatever may be thought of this, in their present form, i. e. as portions of the liturgical collection for the worship of the second temple, all the psalms are post-exilic. Hence even if this psalm be regarded as a poem composed by David, it would still be rash and indicative of ignorance of the history of the Psalter to infer from this passage the existence of an authoritative written Tora long before the exile.

3 The Church fathers Jerome, *Adv. Jovin.* i. 5, [*Opp.* ed. Vallarsi, II. p. 244] and Chrysostom, *Hom. in Matth.* 9, *Opp.* ed. Montfaucon, VII. p. 135 B, already hold that the law-book found in the temple was Deuteronomy. On the basis of this law-book a covenant was concluded by the people with Yahwé; the book was manifestly not laid up again in the temple but copied and disseminated. From the year 621 on Deuteronomy is in a sense the sacred scripture of Israel; in the language of authors subsequent to the reformation of Josiah the evidences of acquaintance with this book are remarkably numerous. It is manifestly the religious standard of the faithful servants of Yahwé in and after the exile down to the coming of Ezra. By the Deuteronomy, perhaps even before the exile, certainly during and after that period, the history of Israel is judged; and by this standard in our books of Judges, Samuel and Kings the whole pre-exilic development is condemned. The promulgation of Deuteronomy is thus the beginning of the canonization of Israel's sacred scriptures (see further § 9).

In the Babylonian exile Israel's spiritual leaders not only devoted themselves zealously to the study of the Mosaic Tora [4], but the extant written prophecies were also much read both for admonition and to strengthen faith [5]. While thus in Babylon between the years 597 and 536 B. C. the foundations for the later canonization of the Tora and Nebiim was already laid, no proof is to be found in the Old Testament that such a collection, clothed with authority, already existed in the exile [6].

[4] When Judah went into exile they took with them in the book of Deuteronomy the written will of God. But by this lawbook itself they were referred to the priests and their tora (Deut. 24, 8. 14, 1 ff.) Whether the priests preserved their toroth in written form or in their memories only, we need not here enquire. Enough that they obviously devoted much study to it and tried to work up the traditional material in various systems. To this we owe the draught of a law by Ezekiel in chapters 40—48; the various groups of laws in the middle books of the Pentateuch, such as Lev. 17—26 and Lev. 1—7; and the whole system of priestly laws in the form in which they were finally introduced after the exile. For our purpose we may leave the question undecided, what in the priestly legislation is old and what is new. It is enough for us for the present to know that in the exile the law was zealously studied. This continued not merely until the return of the first colony in 536, as is obvious from the chapters of Ezekiel which have been cited, but still later. Of Ezra, who returned to Jerusalem in 458, it is narrated that he, who came "with the law of his God in his hand" (Ezra 7, 14. 25), was a priest and a scribe (Neh. 8, 10).

[5] That the writings of the pre-exilic prophets, also, were much read in the exile is easy to understand. The deportation itself would necessarily present itself to the people in the light of a fulfilment of the prophetic warnings. Now they searched the same oracles, which their fathers had spurned, for light in the darkness.

If these had proved themselves truthful in their presages of punishment, they would also in Yahwé's time prove themselves faithful in their predictions of a blessed future. But we do not need to stop with these general observations. We have in the prophecies of Ezekiel and in those of the second Isaiah the proof in hand that the rolls of the ancient men of God were consulted. At every turn Ezekiel, the student, gives evidence of his acquaintance with his predecessors, especially with Isaiah and Jeremiah (Ez. 3, 9. 4, 16 and Jer. 1, 8. 17. 5, 3. Is. 3, 1 &c.). It is the same with the second Isaiah, who in ch. 45, 19—21 appeals to the earlier prophets.

⁶ For the opinion that a collection of prophetic writings existed among the Jews in the exile, appeal might be made to Dan. 9, 2, where Daniel says: "In the first year of his [i. e. Darius'] reign, I, Daniel, observed in the books" &c. From the context it is obvious that among these books were the prophecies of Jeremiah. If the book of Daniel was not written until about 165 B. C. this passage proves nothing more than that in the author's time such a collection of sepharim existed. But even if an earlier date be assigned to the book of Daniel, no inference can be drawn from this passage as to the existence of an authoritative collection.

The period of the restoration of the Jewish people after the exile, or more exactly of the founding of the Jewish church, must be divided into two parts. About the first years after the return under the edict of Cyrus (536) down to the coming of Ezra (458) we are imperfectly informed⁷. There is, however, sufficient reason to believe that the law of Deuteronomy possessed authority among these colonists, and that the writings of the prophets were held in high esteem [8]. In these first 80 years, and indeed even until 445 when Nehemiah came to the aid of Ezra, the situation was not very different from that before and during the exile. Not until 444 did Ezra introduce among his people "The law of his God" which he had brought with him from Babylon. The accounts concerning this in the books of Ezra-Nehemiah admit of no other construction than that at that time canonical authority was secured to the Law, i. e. the Pentateuch [9].

[7] Much interesting information is given to us in Ezra 1—6., including some which might give us to the erroneous impression that the priestly law was already in force before the arrival of Ezra (Ezra 3, 2. 3 and 6, 16). But it should be remembered that the author of the books of Ezra-Nehemiah, who certainly used old memoirs (which however relate to the time after Ezra's coming), lived about 250 B. C., when the priestly law had already been two centuries in authority. Ezra himself was dissatisfied with the condition of things (chap. 9 and 10). The arguments with which König (*Einleitung in das Alte Testament*, 1893, p. 238 f.) combats this position will not hold. Ezra 2 (= Neh. 7) is doubtless older than the time of the author of the book; but it by no means follows that it is earlier than the time of Ezra. It is much more probable that this list belonged to the Memoirs of Nehemiah, and that that champion of the new law, with Ezra, insisted upon the Aaronite descent

of the priests. It is moreover to be observed that this single point does not conclusively prove the supremacy of the priestly *toroth*, since there was undoubtedly a gradual transition in practice between the Deuteronomy and the Priestly law (cf. n. 8).

8 The authority of Deuteronomy appears from the dismissal by Ezra of the foreign wives, which was undertaken solely on the basis of this law (Ezra 10. Deut. 23, 3—5). Of the supremacy of the Priestly law there is no sign. We may indeed find it strange that a larger number of Levites was not ready to return, since Deuteronomy did not exclude them from the service of the altar. But we must reflect that the temple lay in ruins, and that after the introduction of the Deuteronomy a usage had established itself which conceded to the old priestly families of Jerusalem prerogatives which did not to belong to other members of the guild (or tribe) of Levi; cf. *Letterkunde des O. V.*, § 11 n. 7*a*, p. 214, — against König, *op. cit.* p. 238. That the writings of the prophets were held in estimation is sufficiently obvious from the prophecies of Zechariah, who, with Haggai, laboured in this Jewish colony. Reminiscences of older prophets are especially numerous in his book (cf. Zech. 1, 12 with Jer. 25, 11. 12. 29, 10; Zech. 2, 17 with Hab. 2, 20; Zech. 3, 2 with Am. 4, 11 &c.).

9 For our enquiry it is not necessary to decide the question, whether the lawbook introduced by Ezra had been previously known, or whether it was new. The great fact reported to us in Neh 8—10 is that Ezra with the help of Nehemiah got the Tora adopted as a rule of faith and practice, that is, assured for it canonical authority. In the popular assembly "in the street before the Water-gate" at Jerusalem the people bound themselves to live according to the law of Moses; and from the context it is manifest that this law contained various prescriptions which we find in what are, in our judgment, the latest parts of the Pentateuch. (Kuenen, *H. C. O.* I p. 217 = *Hexateuch*

§ 12, note 10). Although certain regulations may have been added subsequently,—such as those about the evening burnt offering (Ex. 29, 38—42), the poll-tax of half a shekel for the sanctuary (Ex. 30, 11—16), and the tithe of cattle (Lev. 27, 32. 33; see § 9, n. 4 and Kuenen *H. C. O.* I. p. 300 f. = *Hexateuch*, § 15, n. 30),—we may say in general that the Sacred Scripture for which Ezra secured normative authority was the Pentateuch. But no more than the Pentateuch. Tradition would ascribe to Ezra more than, this as we shall see later; but it is refuted by various arguments. See also § 9, n. 5.

§ 4.

HISTORICAL EVIDENCE CONCERNING THE CANON OF THE OLD TESTAMENT CONTINUED.

b. IN JEWISH GREEK LITERATURE.

The Jewish books in the Greek language which furnish material for our enquiry cover a period of three centuries, from 200 B. C. (Jesus ben Sirach) to 100 A. D. (Flavius Josephus). The evidence which they give is partly direct, partly indirect.

We have here to consider in the first place the book Σοφία Σείραχ. In the eyes of its author, Jesus ben Sirach of Jerusalem, the Law manifestly stands in very high esteem. He is evidently acquainted with the historical and prophetic books of the Old Testament also; but he draws no definite line of demarcation between his own time and former ages, any more than between the origin of his own work and the inspiration of the prophets[1].

[1] In regard to the date of Jesus ben Sirach, see note [2] of this paragraph. To ascertain what authority the O. T. possessed for him, we must examine the use which he makes of it. It is evident 1. that he exalts the Law very highly (2, 16. 15, 1—8. 19, 20—24. 25, 7—11. 35, 14—16. 35, 23—36, 3. 39, 1 ff.). In ch. 24, 22. 23 wisdom is identified with the Law, and it is evident that for him this is the Sacred Scripture. He is conscious of having obtained all his wisdom through study of the Law. This explains, therefore, 2. the attitude which he takes to the Prophets in the ὕμνος εἰς τοὺς πατέρας (ch. 44—49). He does not see the gulf which separates his own words from those of an Isaiah when he writes (24, 33). "I pour out instruction like prophecy and leave it as a heritage to unending ages." When he has sung the praises of the fathers in ch. 44—49 and passes over to Simon the son of Onias, probably the highpriest of his own time, he shows indeed in the closing verses of this ὕμνος εἰς τοὺς πατέρας (49, 14—16) that he distinguishes the πατέρες from his contemporaries in point of time; but in the eulogy of Simon no specific difference is discoverable. The attitude of Jesus ben Sirach is fully explained if we assume that even in his day the Tora alone had, properly speaking, canonical authority, and that the prophetic scriptures, though undoubtedly held in high esteem, had not yet been declared normative for faith and practice.

§ 4. HISTORICAL EVIDENCE

We have a more direct witness as to the Old Testament Canon in the Prologue of the book Σοφία Σείραχ. This preface was composed by the grandson of the author, who perhaps bore the same name, who translated his grandfather's proverbs into Greek in Egypt, about 132 B. C. Of his grandfather he tells us that he was a zealous student of the Sacred Scriptures, which he thrice speaks of as divided into three groups, ὁ νόμος καὶ οἱ προφῆται (αἱ προφητεῖαι) καὶ οἱ ἄλλοι οἱ κατ' αὐτοὺς ἠκολουθηκότες (τὰ ἄλλα πάτρια βιβλία, τὰ λοιπὰ τῶν βιβλίων) [2].

[2] The time at which Sirach's grandson lived must be determined by the reference which he makes in the preface to the date of his coming to Egypt. He says in regard to this, that it was ἐν τῷ ὀγδόῳ καὶ τριακοστῷ ἔτει ἐπὶ τοῦ Εὐεργέτου βασιλέως. What is meant by the 38th year? Prof. A. Rutgers, in his book *De Echtheid van het tweede gedeelte van Jesaia*, Leiden, 1866, p. 30 ff., endeavours to identify the 38th year with the year 247 B. C. He assumes that "the 38th year" means the 38th year of the era of Dionysius, a celebrated astronomer of Alexandria in the time of Ptolemy Philadelphus, who in honor of his royal patron reckoned the first year of the latter's reign as the first of his era. But however ingeniously developed we cannot admit the theory. It is entirely unproved that this chronology was ever in civil use. The arguments of Prof. de Jong (*de Psalmis Maccabaicis*, Lugd. Bat., 1857, p. 71—74), who fixes the year as 132 B. C., are now pretty generally accepted. The translation was undertaken after 132 B. C. The Euergetes who is named is, therefore, the second of the name, surnamed Physcon, and not, as Rutgers

would have it, Euergetes I (247—221 B. C.). In the former case we obtain for the date of his grandfather about 200; in the latter it would be about 300 B. C. See further Dr. F. E. Daubanton, in *Theol. Studiën*, Utrecht, 1886, p. 238 ff.

We must observe particularly the way in which the author of the Preface refers to a third collection of sacred writings beside the Law and the Prophets. By τὰ ἄλλα πάτρια βιβλία he cannot have meant an indefinite number. But although he may have been well aware what books were included by it, he has not told us, and so has left us in uncertainty.

It is of great importance to determine accurately the value of the testimony which the existence of the Greek version of the Old Testament gives. Inasmuch as it was not completed all at once, but grew up gradually, and we cannot say with certainty when the work was finished, the existence of the LXX does not of itself prove that an authoritative Canon existed before the year 250 B. C.[3]. Furthermore, the manner in which the translators or the earliest readers of the books of the Old Testament treated them, shows that little regard was paid in Alexandria to the idea of canonicity. Though even here the influence of the Palestinian schools cannot be altogether ignored, the addition of apocryphal pieces, and even whole books, which are in no way distinguished from

§ 4. HISTORICAL EVIDENCE

the other writings, shows that the Alexandrians knew no fixed Canon [4].

[3] This is not the place to discuss the origin of the LXX. See, for instance, Dr. J. Z. Schuurmans-Stekhoven, *De Alexandrijnsche vertaling van het Dodekapropheton*, Leiden, 1887, p. 1—5. It is sufficient here merely to recall the fact that according to historical testimony the Law was translated into Greek about 250 B. C. The other books were only gradually translated, and probably for private use. When was this process completed? Sirach's grandson was acquainted, in 132, with a Greek translation of even τὰ ἄλλα πάτρια βιβλία. Were these all Hagiographa of the third section? We do not know. There is a subscription at the close of the translation of the book of Esther: "In the 4th year of the reign of Ptolemy and Cleopatra, Dositheus, who said that he was a priest and Levite, and Ptolemy his son introduced the foregoing epistle concerning *phrourai* (var. *phrouraia* or *phrourim*), which they declared that Lysimachus the son of Ptolemy in Jerusalem had translated." The king Ptolemy referred to is either Ptolemy VI, in which case Esther was already translated in 178, or Ptolemy VIII, in which case this book was not translated until 114 B. C. When Esther had been translated into Greek, the whole O. T., so far as it was in existence, was certainly translated. We see by this subscription that the translation of the other books was made separately. If we assume that Esther was translated as early as 178, Daniel e. g. could not have been translated until afterward. In any case, the existence of the LXX proves nothing in regard to the existence of a fixed Canon of the Jewish Sacred Scriptures.

[4] Judgments differ as to the significance of the well-known fact that in the manuscripts of the LXX other writings are found beside the canonical books, and that the existing books

are enlarged by not unimportant additions. While the LXX contains all the canonical books, it has in addition other compositions of various character. These are either writings which were translated from the Hebrew, such as Jesus Sirach and 1 Maccabees, or supplements and independent books which were evidently composed in Greek. Rightly to estimate this phenomenon we must keep in view the fact that all the manuscripts of the LXX which we possess are of Christian origin, so that in some éven the Magnificat of Mary appears among the hymns. On this account we cannot always say positively whether we have before us the views of the old Alexandrians. In general, however, we doubtless have; for the Christians were in this respect pupils of the Jews, and the apocryphal books are of Jewish origin. We may not, however, infer from this that there existed a divergent Alexandrian Canon. Against this is, 1. the fact that in the various manuscripts the number of apocryphal books varies,—hence no established list existed; 2. the use which Philo makes of the Sacred Scriptures. In support of his teachings he quotes from our canonical books, but never from the apocrypha (see further n. 5 in this §).

While there was, therefore, no fixed Alexandrian Canon, it must not be assumed, on the other hand, that the existence of an official Palestinian Canon was known in Alexandria, as might easily be inferred from what has been said of Philo's use of the Sacred Scriptures. There was undoubtedly constant intercourse between the Palestinian and Alexandrian theologians; even the LXX betrays Palestinian influence. The Law was translated first and most faithfully. This agrees entirely with what we learned from the O. T. about the beginning of canonization. The translation of the Prophets was of later origin, and is already freer; that of the Hagiographa is the freest of all. From this it may reasonably be gathered that the Alexandrian translators themselves held the Nebiim and Kethubim in less exalted esteem than the Tora. The facts are best explained on the assumption that the work of canonization was in progress in Palestine, and that Philo was under the influence of this tendency when for confirmation of his teachings he appeals exclusively to these canonical books.

Among the Jewish Alexandrian writers, Philo (ca. 10 B. C.—50 A. D.) demands special consideration. It is obvious from the use which he made of the Sacred Scriptures of the Old Testament, that he also gave to the Law the highest place; while he entertained such a conception of divine inspiration as to exclude the idea that he accepted an officially defined inspired Canon [5].

[5] Philo of Alexandria may be taken as a type of other Alexandrian Jewish authors. All that we can learn from him in regard to the Canon of the O. T. is comprehended in what has been said in the text. Alexandrian Judaism also gave the Law the highest place, and in this respect Philo does not deviate from his fellow-countrymen. He quotes the Law by far the most frequently; and Moses is to him the source of all wisdom, even that of the Gentiles. Apocryphal books furnish him no proof texts; but it should be remembered that some canonical books are not cited and that in general the Law is the principal arsenal of his *loca probantia*. Philo nowhere quotes from Ezekiel, Daniel, Ecclesiastes, Canticles, Lamentations, Esther, Chronicles, [*] or the Minor Prophets except Hosea and Zechariah.

[*] [But cf. *de congressu* § 8; ed. Mangey I. 525. See B. Pick, "Philo's Canon of the O. T." &c., in *Journal of Biblical Literature* for 1884, 126—143.]

Inspiration, according to him, is by no means confined to the Sacred Scriptures. He regards it as obtainable by any one that practises virtue (*de cherub.* § 14; ed. Mangey, 1742, I. p. 147.)

In a treatise *de vita contemplativa*, attributed to Philo, there appears an allusion to the threefold division of the Canon. It is there (§ 3, II. p. 475) said of the Therapeutae, that they enter their cells with νόμοι καὶ λόγια θεσπισθέντα διὰ προφητῶν καὶ ὕμνοι. It is thought however, upon good grounds, that this tract was written at a later time, probably in the 3d century A. D. (see for instance Kuenen, *Religion of Israel*, London, 1875, II. p. 204). In itself, however, this testimony contains nothing at variance with our other information. Philo may have been acquainted with the three divisions of the Old Testament scriptures as well as the author of the preface to the Book of Sirach.

Of somewhat earlier date, i. e. from the close of the first century B. C., is an account of a collection of Jewish sacred books in 2 Macc. 2, 13, which runs as follows: ἐξηγοῦντο δὲ καὶ ἐν ταῖς ἀναγραφαῖς καὶ τοῖς ὑπομνηματισμοῖς τοῖς κατὰ τὸν Νεεμίαν τὰ αὐτά, καὶ ὡς καταβαλλόμενος βιβλιοθήκην ἐπισυνήγαγε τὰ περὶ τῶν βασιλέων καὶ προφητῶν [Α βιβλία] καὶ τὰ τοῦ Δαυιδ καὶ ἐπιστολὰς βασιλέων περὶ ἀναθεμάτον. If this statement is trustworthy, it follows from it that Nehemiah had performed a useful service in collecting sacred books and other important documents, but not that he had any part in the canonization of the Old Testament books [6].

[6] The Second Book of Maccabees begins with two letters, 1. ch. 1, 1—9 written by "the Jews in Jerusalem and the country places of Judaea, to the brethren in Egypt" in the year 188, (of the Seleucid era, = 124 B. C.); and 2. ch. 1, 10—2, 18, sent by "the inhabitants of Jerusalem and Judaea and the Council and Judas, to Aristobulus, the instructor of King Ptolemy, who is of the stock of the anointed priests, and to the Jews in Egypt." For proof of the spuriousness of both letters, which were probably interpolated later in 2 Maccabees, see, for instance, Joh. Dyserinck, *De Apocriefe Boeken des Ouden Verbonds*, Haarlem 1874, p. 77; Schürer, *Gesch. d. Jüd. Volkes*, u. s. w. II. p. 741 = *Hist. of the Jewish People*, 2d Div., Vol. III. p. 244; and C. Bruston in Stade's *Z. A. T. W.*, 1890, p. 110 ff., who discovers in 1, 1—9 two letters (vs. 1—6; 7—9). It is hard to determine the age of these letters; it can only be said that they suppose the existence of the temple in Jerusalem, and thus must have been written before 70 A. D. Probably they do not differ much in date from the book to which they are prefixed.

In treating of Solomon's sacrifice at the dedication of the temple, which is said to have been consumed by fire from heaven, the author informs us that this was also related in the ἀναγραφαὶ καὶ ὑπομνηματισμοὶ οἱ κατὰ τὸν Νεεμίαν. In this (probably pseudepigraphic) production, which was thus in circulation in Alexandria in the first century B. C., it was further narrated "that Nehemiah founded a library, and collected for it the narratives about the kings and the prophets, and the writings of David, and the letters of [foreign] princes concerning gifts to the temple."

It may seem to some rash to pick out any historical fact from these spurious letters, full as they are of legends and fables; nevertheless, it appears to me that we come here upon a fact which may very well be explained as historical, and fitted into a history of the Old Testament Canon. We observe, 1. that the author of the letter did not invent the story, but found it in an older book. This book cannot be a mere fiction of the author, but must have really existed; otherwise he would have needlessly imperilled the credibility of his letters. 2. It does not, of course, follow from this that what is related of Nehemiah in this older book is historical; but it should not escape our attention that Nehemiah is here named, and that his work is spoken of in terms that inspire confidence. In the first century B. C., when the Law had for four centuries possessed canonical authority, and even the Prophets had for nearly two centuries shared the same, a collection of books περὶ τῶν βασιλέων καὶ προφητῶν would certainly, unless there had been some historical basis for the story, have been attributed to Ezra and not to Nehemiah, and in different terms from those in which it is here done. 3. What we are here told of Nehemiah may be brought into accord with what we know of him from the O. T., viz. that he compiled genealogical rolls [7, 5 ff.].

It is scarcely possible to identify the writings here named with our Nebiim and Kethubim. All that can be inferred from the story is that in the first century B. C. a tradition was current in Alexandria about Nehemiah, that he, not as a scribe with the intention of forming a canon, but as a lover of books, founded a library; and that he collected letters concerning gifts (probably of Persian kings) to the temple, and perhaps gave them to the priests, that they might on occasion appeal to them. In this he may have followed the example of the Persian kings and of Hezekiah (Prov. 25, 1). Possibly the expression τὰ τοῦ Δαυιδ may refer to a first collection of liturgical poems of which the greater part are still extant in our Psalter in Ps. 3—41, to which the last verse of Ps. 72 was the original close.

In 2 Macc. 2, 14 we read, "In like manner Judas also collected all the books which were scattered during the war which we had." This statement may very well be worthy of credence; but yields us nothing for the history of canonization, for we are not told what these books were. The Tora had then for three centuries been regarded as canonical; the Prophets were doubtless already regarded as a closed collection; and what influence Judas' collection had upon the canonization of the Kethubim cannot possibly be gathered from the passage. The only thing which we may learn from this verse, is, that in spite of the destruction of many manuscripts by Antiochus Epiphanes, by the care of Judas the Maccabee many precious documents were saved.

From a Jewish apocalypse written about the close of the first century A. D., the so called 4 (2) Esdras (14, 18—47 [Engl. vers. 19—48]), it is evident that toward the end of the first century of our era in Jewish circles a Canon of twenty four books was recognized, and that gradually the part which Ezra had in the canonization of the Old Testament, viz. giving binding force to the Tora, was being extended to the entire Old Testament [7].

[7] This book, which in the Latin Church is known as 4 Esdras [in the English Bible, 2 Esdras] is called by the fathers, who are manifestly much influenced by it, Ἔσδρας ὁ προφήτης (Clem. Alex., *Strom.* iii. 16 [ed. Potter, I. p. 556]) or Ἔσδρα

ἀποκάλυψις. It was written toward the end of the first century A. D., whether under Nerva, 97 A. D. (Volkmar, Langen, Hausrath, Renan), or under Domitian, 81—96 A. D. (Gfrörer, Dillmann, Wieseler, Reuss)*. This strange book was much read in the ancient Church, as appears from the translations from the original Greek (which save for a few fragments is lost) into Latin, Syriac, Aethiopic, Arabic and Armenian. What many of the church fathers say about the O. T. Canon is very obviously based upon this fable. In the Middle Ages also the book was still much in vogue, and even found admission into the Protestant Zürich Version of the Bible of the year 1530 and into the English Bible. The contents of the passage with which we are concerned are substantially as follows: Ezra asks before his death that God will illumine him by his Spirit so that he may write down for posterity all that has happened in the world from the beginning, and what God is still to do, as it was written in the Law which had been burned (vs. 18—22). He receives command to seclude himself for forty days and to take with him five skilful penmen, &c. (vs. 23—26). He now reminds the Israelites, how by their own fault they had lost the Law which they had received at the exodus from Egypt, and commands them to leave him alone during forty days (vs. 27—36). After a seclusion of forty days, Ezra betakes himself with his five assistants to the open country; a cup is offered to him, and when he has drained it he begins to speak continuously for forty days and nights (vs. 37—43). A great number of books is thus produced (vs. 44, 46). One text has 974, various others 904, 94, 84. The Oriental versions all have 94. Seventy of these books Ezra is to deliver to the wise men

---

*[See Schürer, *G. J. V.*, II. p. 646 ff. = *Hist. Jewish People &c.* 2d Div. Vol. III. p. 93 ff.; Kabisch *Das vierte Buch Esra auf seine Quellen untersucht*, 1889.]

of his people; the remainder (i. e. 24) he is to publish. The intention is plain. The 24 books are well-known writings; among the 70 others must be classed 4 (2) Esdras itself, which was not to be revealed until a later time. We have here, therefore, unambiguous testimony that in Jewish circles at the close of the first century A. D. the number of canonical books was computed at 24.

It is remarkable how clearly the development of tradition is reflected in this apocalypse. At the outset the narrative speaks only of the Law, which Israel had received at the exodus from Egypt (vs. 27—36) and which had been burned [in the destruction of Jerusalem by Nebuchadnezzar], expressing thus the genuine tradition, supported by well attested historical evidence, that Ezra had a great part in the writing down and introduction of the Law. But as he goes on the author quietly extends the sphere of Ezra's efforts over the entire O. T. In this respect he evidently represents the intellectual drift of Judaism in his days.

The last but not the least important witness among the Jewish Greek authors is the historian Flavius Josephus. Both directly and indirectly he bears witness to the Hellenistic views about the Old Testament Canon. This explains both the fact that in his celebrated historical work, *Archaeologia Judaica*, he makes use of apocryphal as well as of the canonical books, and, on the other hand, that in his controversial treatise *Contra Apionem* i. 8 (written about 100 A. D.) he gives the number of canonical books as twenty-two, and manifestly combines them in the Alexandrian manner. As to the closing of the Canon he gives no definite account; but he gives us clearly to understand by what standard the canonicity of the books is to be judged [8].

[8] It appears to me that Flavius Josephus is a genuine representative of the Alexandrian views about the O. T. Canon. What I understand by this, my readers already know. I mean to say that he does not take the idea of canonical scripture very strictly. But when he is questioned about it or is obliged to defend his Jewish stand-point, he has no other answer than that which the Palestinian scribes would give. In principle, therefore, he occupies the same stand-point as Philo, who for his *loca probantia* quotes from no other than the canonical scriptures.

This explains the fact that in the "Antiquities" he gives a very broad sense to the term Holy Scriptures, as e. g. in the Procemium § 3, where it is said that the history of 5000 years is comprised in τὰ ἱερὰ γράμματα. The very broadest sense is given to it when he says (xx. 11, 2) that he has written the entire history, down to the 12th year of Nero, ὡς αἱ ἱεραὶ βίβλοι περὶ πάντων ἔχουσι τὴν ἀναγραφήν. But here the rhetorician is speaking, not the historian.

Over against this broad view stands the important passage *contra Apionem* i. 8, [Text of Niese]: Οὐ μυριάδες βιβλίων εἰσὶ παρ' ἡμῖν ἀσυμφώνων καὶ μαχομένων, δύο δὲ μόνα πρὸς τοῖς εἴκοσι βιβλία τοῦ παντὸς ἔχοντα χρόνου τὴν ἀναγραφήν, τὰ δικαίως * πεπιστευμένα. Καὶ τούτων πέντε μέν ἐστι Μωυσέως· ἃ τούς τε νόμους περιέχει καὶ τὴν ἀπ' ἀνθρωπογονίας παράδοσιν μέχρι τῆς

---

* Eusebius adds θεῖα, which on both internal and external ground is to be rejected. [See Eichhorn, *Einleitung* [4], I. 144 n.]

αὑτοῦ τελευτῆς· οὗτος ὁ χρόνος ἀπολείπει τρισχιλίων ὀίγῳ ἐτῶν. Ἀπὸ δὲ τῆς Μωυσέως τελευτῆς μέχρι τῆς Ἀρταξέρξου τοῦ μετὰ Ξέρξην Περσῶν βασιλέως οἱ μετὰ Μωυσῆν προφῆται τὰ κατ' αὑτοὺς πραχθέντα συνέγραψαν ἐν τρισὶ καὶ δέκα βιβλίοις· αἱ δὲ λοιπαὶ τέσσαρες ὕμνους εἰς τὸν θεὸν καὶ τοῖς ἀνθρώποις ὑποθήκας τοῦ βίου περιέχουσιν. Ἀπὸ δὲ Ἀρταξέρξου μέχρι καθ' ἡμᾶς χρόνου γέγραπται μὲν ἕκαστα, πίστεως δὲ οὐχ ὁμοίας ἠξίωται τοῖς πρὸ αὐτῶν διὰ τὸ μὴ γενέσθαι τὴν τῶν προφητῶν ἀκριβῆ διαδοχήν. Δῆλον δ' ἐστὶν ἔργῳ, πῶς ἡμεῖς πρόσιμεν* τοῖς ἰδίοις γράμμασι· τοσούτου γὰρ αἰῶνος ἤδη παρῳχηκότος οὔτε προσθεῖναί τις οὐδὲν οὔτε ἀφελεῖν αὐτῶν οὔτε μεταθεῖναι τετόλμηκεν, πᾶσι δὲ σύμφυτόν ἐστιν εὐθὺς ἐκ πρώτης γενέσεως· Ἰουδαίοις τὸ νομίζειν αὐτὰ θεοῦ δόγματα καὶ τούτοις ἐμμένειν καὶ ὑπὲρ αὐτῶν, εἰ δέοι, θνήσκειν ἡδέως.

We observe in this narrative three things of importance to our enquiry: 1. Josephus fixes the number of the books at 22; 2. he combines them after the Alexandrian fashion; 3. he assumes a standard for the canonicity of books which in every way deserves our attention. Upon each of these points we must speak somewhat more in particular. 1. Josephus classifies, the O. T. books as the five of Moses, thirteen of the prophets and four of hymns and maxims for human life. The total 22 can only be obtained by supposing that Ruth and Lamentations are included among the 13 prophets. The most probable hypothesis, especially in view of Josephus' conception of the διαδοχὴ τῶν προφητῶν (see below, on 3), is that he connected Ruth with Judges, and Lamentations with Jeremiah. The number 22 is unalterably fixed. Josephus declares that, although so long a time had intervened since they were written, no one had ever ventured to add anything to these scriptures, or to take

---

* [So Euseb., Niese: others, with the Ms., τοῖς ἰδίοις γράμμασι πεπιστεύκαμεν.]

from them, or to make any change in them &c. 2. As is obvious from what has already been adduced, Josephus puts the books together in the Alexandrian way. He must have counted Chronicles, Ezra and Nehemiah, and Daniel among the thirteen prophets, that is to say, historical books; for they cannot belong among the four books of "hymns and maxims for life." The four last named probably consisted of "David" (Psalms) and "Solomon" (Proverbs, Ecclesiastes, Canticles). The book of Job is treated by him as an historical book and numbered among the thirteen prophets. We call this the Alexandrian way of combining the books, because, with numerous variations, it appears in the manuscripts of the LXX. The fact that Josephus names David and Solomon last does not indicate that he would have placed them last in a complete collection of the O. T. books; he mentions them separately because they do not contain history. 3. Josephus presupposes a standard for the canonicity of the 22 books of which he speaks. He says that from the time of Artaxerxes down to his own everything had been recorded, but that these records were not deemed worthy of equal confidence, because since Artaxerxes the regular succession of prophets had ceased. Josephus's meaning is not doubtful. He regards the prophets as the writers of the history of their own times. In the reign of Artaxerxes I he (erroneously) dates the story of Esther (*Antt.* xi. 6, 13), and puts Ezra-Nehemiah (as mistakenly) under Xerxes (*Antt.* xi. 5, 1 ff.). It is evident from this that he regards the author of Esther as the last in the series of the thirteen prophets. Now it must be carefully noted that Josephus is dealing only with the credibility of the prophetic historical books of the Bible, and says nothing about their canonicity or inspiration (cf. Kuenen, *H. K. O.*[1], III. p. 425). Nevertheless these books (by us called canonical) not only stand on a higher plane than other books of history, but from childhood the Jews esteem them as θεοῦ δόγματα "in which they desire to abide, and for which they are ready, if need be, to die gladly." The divine light in which the men of prophecy viewed and described the events of their time and of which the credibility of their writings was a consequence, through the διαδοχή makes this number of books as it were a whole. If at a later time divine inspiration fell to the lot of others, they have left no writings that could be received into this series. Josephus thus does not say that the Canon was closed by the last prophet; he does not think it necessary. The series *was* closed, and the fact did not require to be officially proclaimed.

My impression is that Josephus' view, along with much that is untenable—e. g. about the "succession of prophets," a theory which is also found in Jewish sources (cf. § 6 n. 3 and Buhl, *Kanon u. Text*, p. 35; Eng. tr. p. 36)—contains important elements of historic truth. These elements are, 1. That the line between canonical and uncanonical coincides, in the thought of Josephus and the circle of which he is a representative, with the cessation of prophecy; and 2. that a general settled persuasion in regard to canonicity precedes the decision of the schools. We shall see in fact, in § 6, that in the days of Josephus the schools still had their doubts about certain books of the third division. But among the people there existed in his days such a reverence for precisely the books which still constitute our Canon (as the number given by Josephus proves) that "if need be they would gladly die for them."

§ 5.

HISTORICAL EVIDENCE CONCERNING THE CANON OF THE OLD TESTAMENT CONTINUED.

c. IN THE NEW TESTAMENT.

The indirect evidence regarding the Old Testament Canon in the New Testament is sufficiently important to be separately considered by us, especially as Christian theologians. How little support it lends to the theories which have been adopted from Jewish scholars will be manifest in this paragraph.

The Old Testament is quoted in the New as "the Scripture," "the Scriptures," "the Holy Scriptures," "the Law and the Prophets," or simply as "the Law"[1]. In one instance only (Luk. 24, 44) language is used which points to a three-fold division; but it can not by any means be proved by this that in this place a Canon is intended, still less one of the same extent as ours[2]. It has also been asserted, but not proved, that the words of Matth. 23, 35 presuppose the existence of our Canon[3].

[1] In regard to the names by which the Old Testament as a whole is designated, the following facts are to be observed:

§ 5. HISTORICAL EVIDENCE

Ἡ γραφή occurs e. g. John 10, 35. 19, 36. 2 Pet. 1, 20; αἱ γραφαί Matt. 22, 29. Acts. 18, 24, γραφαὶ ἅγιαι Rom. 1, 2; ἱερὰ γράμματα 2 Tim. 3, 15, &c. These names need no comment; but they leave us in entire uncertainty as to the limits of the Canon. Moreover where the expression ἡ γραφή is used, it does not always refer to the Holy Scriptures as a whole. It may often denote the scripture passage, the passage from the Sacred Scriptures. In Jo. 10, 35 however it certainly denotes the Scriptures as a whole, though what is comprised in them is not indicated. (Cf. C. Sepp, *De Leer des N. V. over de Heilige Schrift des Ouden Verbonds*, Amsterdam, 1849, p. 69 ff.). The name νόμος καὶ προφῆται, which occurs frequently (Matt. 5, 17. 7, 12. 22, 40. Luk. 16, 16. 29. 31. Acts 13, 15. 28, 23), is somewhat more definite. But neither from this appellation can anything be gathered as to the extent of the Canon. The assumption that the προφῆται must include the Hagiographa is quite unproved. It is equally erroneous, however, to infer from this appellation that the third division of the Old Testament was not regarded by the N. T. writers as sacred. It must not be forgotten that in the passages cited there is no reference to a canon of books, but to the *old dispensation*, which may very properly be comprehensively designated by the name "the Law and the Prophets." Or, if more prominence is given to the Scriptures which acquaint us with this dispensation, then the two divisions are named which possessed the greatest authority and which do more to teach us the will of God than any book of the third division. Above all it should not escape our attention that the whole of the O. T. Scriptures is more than once called ὁ νόμος, John 10, 34. 12, 34. 15, 25. 1 Cor. 14, 21. This is the more remarkable because in all the three passages cited from the Fourth Gospel texts from the Prophets or the Psalms are intended; while 1 Cor. 14, 21 very clearly refers to Is. 28, 11, and can only with difficulty be brought into connection with Dt. 28, 49. The significance of this fact will fully appear in § 8.

² It is not surprising that Luk. 24, 44, where ὁ νόμος καὶ οἱ προφῆται καὶ ψαλμοί are named, should have been looked upon as a proof that the New Testament writers were acquainted with the threefold division of the O. T. Canon. It must then be assumed that οἱ ψαλμοί alone are named, as the most important part of the Kethubim, but that the other books of the third part are in the author's mind included with them. But the context must be consulted, and no violence done to the plain sense of the words. The meaning must be derived from the text, not imported into it. What does the context teach? The risen Lord is trying to make clear to his disciples, as he had to the pilgrims to Emmaus (vs. 26. 27), that the Christ must suffer and must rise from the dead on the third day. They were to learn this from the Scriptures. Now what book of the third division could be adduced for this purpose except simply and solely the book of Psalms? Luk. 24, 44 teaches us, consequently, that in the days of Jesus not only the Law and the Prophets were esteemed sacred, but other books besides, among them especially the Psalms.

³ It has been thought that evidence of the existence of the complete Old Testament Canon in Jesus' time might be derived from Matt. 23, 35 (cf. Luk. 11, 51) (Riehm in *Handwörterbuch des Biblischen Alterthums*, 1884, p. 1318, art. "Sacharja.") The case stands thus: The Lord says there, "That upon you may come all the righteous blood shed on the earth, from the blood of righteous Abel unto the blood of Zachariah son of Barachiah, whom ye slew between the temple and the altar." Now the last martyr of the O. T. is not this Zachariah ben Jehoiada, who was murdered under Joash (9th century B. C.), but Uriah ben Shemaiah, under Jehoiakim in the 7th century B. C. (Jer. 26, 23). Had Jesus therefore had in mind the order of

time, it is argued, he would have said, from Abel to Uriah. Why then does he say, from Abel to Zachariah? Because Zachariah is named last in the O. T. (2 Chron. 24, 20. 21). Jesus' language is therefore, it is asserted, as much as to say, the blood of all the righteous named throughout the entire Scripture, or as we should say "from Genesis to Revelation." It would follow from this, that in the O. T. as Jesus had it before him Chronicles was the last book as, it is in our own Hebrew Bible.

It must be remembered, however, that scarcely any one in those days possessed a complete collection of the Holy Scriptures; most of the synagogues even were not so rich. And if any one had the mall, the rolls were all separate. At most, therefore, the words could only signify that the Lord embraced the same theory about the sequence of these books which is formulated in the Massora. But even granting this, it follows only that Jesus, like the later Jews, regarded Chronicles as the last in the series of O. T. books. *What* books were then ascribed to this third collection which is closed by Chronicles, Matt. 23, 35 does not tell us at all. But furthermore, is it not much more probable that the Lord had in mind the series of historical books in the narrower sense, to which Jeremiah did not belong, and among which the book of Chronicles has always been esteemed the youngest and last? We have thus done full justice to this passage, and have left out of account the hypothesis that the words are to be explained as a mere inaccurary, or that Zachariah ben Baruch is meant, who was killed at Jerusalem in the Jewish war. (See Oort, *Laatste Eeuwen*, enz., II. p. 353 ff.). Matt. 23, 35, where Zachariah is called "the son of Barachiah," is certainly incorrect. This is, at least according to Zach. 1, 1 (cf. Is. 8, 2. Ezra 5, 1), a confusion with the post-exilic prophet of this name. In the parallel passage Luk. 11, 51. the addition "the son of Barachiah" is lacking.

It is probably not altogether accidental that in the New Testament there are no quotations from the books of Esther, Ecclesiastes and Canticles [4]. And a number of reminiscences and quotations from apocryphal writings prove very certainly that the New Testament writers recognized no Canon of the Old Testament agreeing with ours [5].

[4] There is of course always room for the opinion that it is to be imputed entirely to accident that the books of Esther, Ecclesiastes, Canticles, and likewise Ezra, Nehemiah, Obadiah, Nahum, and Zephaniah are nowhere quoted. Yet in view of the character of most of these books the fact does not surprise us; the matter is put, moreover, in a different light by what we know from Jewish and Christian sources about some of these books. See further § 6, n. 5 and 6 and § 7 n. 1, 3, 4. The absence of quotations from Ezra-Nehemiah has but little significance, because these books were originally one with Chronicles, although in Jesus's days perhaps already divided. The same is true also of Obadiah, Nahum, and Zephaniah, from which there are no quotations, inasmuch as these writings are subdivisions of the one Dodekapropheton.

[5] The fact that the N. T. writers quote from apocryphal books can only be denied by dogmatic prejudice. (See besides the N. T. commentaries the well-known work of G. Surenhusius, ספר המשוה, *sive* βίβλος καταλλαγῆς, *in quo secundum veterum theologorum Hebraeorum formulas allegandi, et modos interpretandi conciliantur loca ex V. in N. T. allegata*, Amstelaedami, 1713). The facts speak too plainly, and it is a hopeless undertaking to try to invalidate them. On the other side their significance was no doubt at one time exaggerated; for example by E. R. Stier ("Sogar die Apocryphen im N. T." in his *Andeu-*

§ 5. HISTORICAL EVIDENCE.

tungen für gläubiges Schriftverständniss, 2e Sammlung, 1828, p. 486—520), who collected no less than 102 passages in the N. T. which exhibited some resemblance to the apocrypha. Bleek ("Ueber die Stellung der Apocryphen d. A. T. im Christlichen Kanon," *Studien und Kritiken*, 1853, p. 267—354) cut down the number very much. (p. 336 ff.). We should discriminate, 1. reminiscences of apocryphal writings; 2. information derived from apocryphal sources and treated in the same way with narratives from the O. T.; and 3. actual quotations.

Thus, 1. Rom. 1, 20—32 is merely a reminiscence of Wisdom of Solomon ch. 13—15; 1 Cor. 6, 13 of Sirach 36, 20; Heb. 1, 3 of Wisdom 7, 26; Jas. 1, 9 of Sirach 4, 29 and 5, 11; 1 Pet. 1, 6. 7 of Wisdom 3, 3—7. These passages therefore prove no more than that the respective apocryphal texts were probably in the mind of the writers. The second class must be deemed of more significance, in which the N. T. authors relate things which they can only have derived from apocryphal sources and put them in the same rank with events narrated in the O. T. Thus in 2 Tim. 3, 8 the Egyptian sorcerers Jannes and Jambres are mentioned, names which appear in various forms in the Targums and Talmud also (in the Talmud יוחני וממרא; in the Targum of Jonathan [Ex. 1, 15. 7, 11] ינים וימברים), and must have been derived from a lost book on the times of Moses. Heb. 11, 34. 35 alludes to the story in 2 Macc. 6, 18—7, 42; Heb. 11, 37 to a passage from the *Martyrium Jesaiae*. Jude vs. 9 also is derived from the *Assumptio Mosis*. 3. Of the greatest weight are the direct quotations. These are found in Matt. 27, 9. Luk. 11, 49. John 7, 38. 1 Cor. 2, 9. Eph. 5, 14 and Jude vs. 14—16. On each of these passages a brief note. In Matt. 27, 9 the name *Jeremiah* is not a lapsus calami. The same passage which we should look for in Zech. 11, 12 was quoted by the author of the first Gospel from an apocryphal book of Jeremiah. Jerome says in his commentary on this passage, "Legi nuper in quodam Hebraico volumine, quod Nazarenae sectae mihi Hebraeus obtulit, Jeremiae apocryphum, in quo haec ad verbum scripta reperi" (*Opp.* ed. Vallarsi, VII. p. 228; see Schürer, *Geschichte des Jüd. Volkes*, u. s. w., II. p. 676 = *Hist. of the Jewish People*, 2d Div. III. p. 132). — Luk. 11, 49. John 7, 38 and Jac. 4, 5 are manifestly quotations, although we are not able to identify the sources. We can hardly imagine with Hugo Grotius (see his commentary), that εἶπε in Luk. 11, 49 is equivalent to אמר בלבו, he thought. God thought thus; for thus it came to pass! The explanation of A. Resch *Aussercanonische Evangelienfragmente*, Leipzig, 1889, § 10, sub no. 4, must also be rejected. — 1 Cor. 2, 9 is derived, according to Origen, from the "Apocalypse of Elias," and so also, according to Epiphanius, is Eph. 5, 14. Resch (*op. cit*, § 10, sub no. 37), on very slender grounds, makes these passages words of Jesus. — Finally, in Jude vs. 14 — 16 the prophecy of Enoch the seventh from Adam is derived from the apocryphal book of Enoch. On all the apocrypha mentioned, in connection also with the N. T. passages, see Schürer, *Geschichte d. Jüd. Volkes* u. s. w. II. 575 — 693 = *Hist. of the Jewish People*, &c. 2d Div. III. p. 1—155.

The fullest light should be allowed to fall upon all of these facts. It then appears, 1. that many passages from apocryphal writings were present to the mind of the N. T. authors, which they often accorded equal weight with texts from the O. T. 2. The apocrypha in question are not even those of the LXX; for precisely in the actual quotations (see above, 3) writings are used which are not found in the manuscripts of the LXX. 3. It is manifest from this that most of the N. T. writers gave to the notion of "Sacred Scripture" an even wider range than most of the Alexandrians [*].

---

[*] Ryle (*Canon of the O. T.*, p. 153 ff.) will not admit the force of these passages. He thinks that some quotations (such as Jo. 7, 38. 1 Cor. 2, 9)

§ 5. HISTORICAL EVIDENCE

While thus, on the one hand, the evidence of the New Testament itself annuls the hypothesis that from the days of Ezra there existed a fixed Canon, which was recognized by Jesus and his apostles [6], on the other hand it affords us some positive suggestions for the formation of our own theory of the history of canonization [7].

---

[6] That the Lord and his apostles accepted our Canon as authoritative has been recently reaffirmed by M. Noordtzij, *de Leer van Jezus en de Apostelen over de H. S. des O. T.*, Kampen, 1886. See on the other side my criticism in the *Theol. Studiën*, 1886, p. 156—163, which may be supplemented at some points from this paragraph.

Dr. Ed. Böhl has attempted in another way to explain the fact that the N. T. writers evidently follow the LXX in preference to the Massoretic text, a point closely connected with the use of the apocrypha. In his *Forschungen nach einer Volksbibel zur Zeit Jesu*, u. s. w., Wien, 1873, Böhl maintains that the LXX had found so much acceptance in Palestine that an Aramaic translation of it had been made, and that this was used by Jesus and his apostles. The second part of this work appeared in 1875, under the title *Die Alttestamentlichen Citate im N. T.* In it

---

"are to be explained as giving the substance and combined thought of more than one passage of the Old Testament," and that it is not proved that Matt. 27, 9. Lu. 11, 49 are derived from an apocryphal book. The testimony of the Church fathers seems to us to outweigh the dogmatic judgments of the English Professor. Let the reader put his argument by the side of ours and ask himself which view is the more probable. This further may be remarked, that the formula of citation, εἶπε, is the common one in quoting from the Scriptures, — שאמר in the rabbinical literature.

he tries to prove that the O. T. quotations in the N. T. are taken from the Aramaic. The existence of such an Aramaic translation is wholly unproved. And we are to believe that this translation was inspired, and hence the authorized word of God for that time! What assumptions will men not make to uphold a weak hypothesis!

In his *Christologie des A. T.*, p. 305, Böhl says in regard to Matt. 27, 9: "In the vernacular Bible which he used, Matthew found this passage from Zechariah in Jeremiah, probably appended to Jer. 19, 15, We no longer find it in Jeremiah, but in the prophecy of Zechariah, which thus becomes in a certain sense a *fons secundarius* for this important incident."

We may safely put this opinion in the same category with that of the Jesuit Harduin (died 1729), who in his Commentary on the N. T. imagined that Latin was the original tongue of the N. T. He believed (mistakenly, at least as regards the Eastern regions) that Latin was better known in all provinces of the Roman empire than Greek; and that God, who foresaw that the Latin language would ere long become still more universal, for this reason probably inspired the N. T. in that language! — Such hypotheses really need only to be stated, not refuted. See, however, a conclusive criticism upon Böhl's *Forschungen*, by Prof. Kuenen in the *Theol. Tijdschrift*, 1874, p. 207—212.

7 The positive suggestions which the N. T. offers us for our enquiry are not many, but they are weighty. It is apparent from what has been said above (p. 51 ff.), 1. that in the Jewish circles from which Jesus and his apostles came, a very broad conception of Holy Scriptures was entertained. The early Christians did not depart from it. A whole list of apocrypha is actually of Christian origin (see Schürer). 2. There are traces, however, of a more restricted signification. For the names given to the Holy Scriptures (see this §, n. 1) can hardly be applied

to apocrypha; while it is generally obvious from the connexion in which they appear that in fact only books which are contained in our Canon are meant. 3. All the facts are explained by the hypothesis that in Jesus' days the competent authorities had not yet defined the Canon; that only the Law and the Prophets enjoyed undisputed authority; that beside the Psalms, Daniel, and other books of the Kethubim, many apocryphal writings also were freely read; but that over against this the schools were beginning to restrict and regulate their use. To this authority of the schools the Lord and his disciples would readily submit (Matt. 23, 2. 3), and if questioned would have given an answer not very different from the later Jewish enumeration. We have already seen that the same shifting point of view is still to be observed in Josephus.

§ 6.

HISTORICAL EVIDENCE CONCERNING THE CANON OF THE OLD TESTAMENT CONTINUED.

d. IN PALESTINIAN JEWISH SOURCES, ESPECIALLY IN THE TALMUD.

In the nature of the case, in our investigation of the history of the Old Testament Canon, following in the footsteps of Christian theologians since the days of Jerome, we must give attentive consideration to the Jewish statements. We are all the more bound to do so when we perceive that the opinions adopted from Jewish scholars in the 16th century evince but slight agreement with the various statements in the Talmud and other sources [1].

[1] That we devote a separate paragraph to the Jewish evidence concerning the O. T. Canon surely requires no further explanation. A critical examination of this evidence is not only necessary on its own account, but is demanded by other considerations. Christian theologians in former times rightly sought the light they needed for the correct understanding of the O. T. among the Jews. But they frequently adopted without criticism what Jewish scholars in their turn accepted without criticism. Thus the opinion of which we have already spoken in our Introductory Remarks (n. 1) universally prevailed, namely, that as early as Ezra's time the whole Canon of the O. T. was definitely fixed. We read how Hottinger with the utmost assurance declares (*Thesaurus philologicus* i. 2, *quaest.* 1) "Inconcussum enim hactenus, et tam apud Christianos* quam Judaeos ἀναμφισβήτον fuit principium, simul et semel Canonem V. T. authoritate prorsus divina constitutum esse ab Esdra et viris Synagogae magnae." It will be made evident that this theory of the Jewish scholars is no established tradition, but an hypothesis, based upon various pieces of evidence, which when properly interpreted contain something quite different. Elias Levita († 1549) and David Kimchi († 1240) are only derived and turbid sources. We must first of all review the Talmudic statements themselves.

* "Inter eos quibus non pro cerebro fungus est," he says in another place.

In the first place it must be noted that in the Talmud, both in the Gemara (ca. 500 A. D.) and in the Mishna (ca. 200 A. D.), the existence of our Canon and its division into Tora, Nebiim and Kethubim are everywhere taken for granted ².

² About this there is no difference of opinion. Cases in which proof texts are cited from all three divisions of the Old Testament scriptures may be found in Surenhusius, *op cit.*, p. 49 f., *Thesis xi:* "Ad majorem rei confirmationem aliquando Mosis, Prophetarum, et Hagiographorum verba allegantur........ Interdum addi solent haec verba דבר זה כתוב בתורה שנויה בנביאים משולש בכתובים, res haec scripta est in Lege, iterata in Prophetis, et tertio in Hagiographis."

Not in regard to the canonization, but in regard to the writers and editors of the Old Testament books, strange theories are propounded in the Babylonian Talmud (*Baba Bathra* fol. 14*b*, 15*a*) ³.

³ That some (e. g. Herzfeld, *Geschichte des Volkes Israel*, II. p. 94, and Fürst, *Kanon*, p. 129—134) have thought that this well-known passage treats of the canonization of scripture is due to the fact that they ascribe all sorts of meanings to the verb כתב. Herzfeld and, substantially, Fürst*, suppose that כתב in the Talmud means, 1. to commit oral traditions to writing;

* [See also König, *Einleitung*, p. 445.]

2. to collect the words or writings of others; 3. to write, or compose a book; 4. to incorporate a book in the Canon. But this verb has no other meaning than 'write, compose a book.' This will be clearly evident when we present the passage in its entirety.

The passage in question is not a Mishna, but a Baraitha accompanied by an extended Gemara. Text, translation, and commentary may be found in the little work of G. A. Marx [Dalman] which has been mentioned above, *Traditio rabbinorum veterrima*, etc. On the difference between Baraitha and Mishna, see Strack, *Einleitung in den Thalmud*, Leipzig, 1887, p. 5 f. (= *P. R. E²*., XVIII. p. 297 f. art. "Thalmud").

We present here only the translation of the Baraitha as given by Marx (p. 20 f.) and at the close as much of the Gemara as is necessary to a correct understanding: "Magistri nostri docent: Ordo Prophetarum hic est: Josua, Judicum, Samuelis, Regum, Jeremias, Ezechiel, Jesajas, Duodecim......" "Ordo Hagiographorum hic est: Ruth, liber Psalmorum, Jobus et Proverbia, Ecclesiastes, Canticum Canticorum et Threni, Daniel et libellus Esther, Ezra et Chronica ......"

"Quis autem scripsit eos libros? Mose scripsit librum suum et sectionem de Bileamo et Jobum. Josua scripsit librum suum et octo illos versus in Lege. Samuel scripsit librum suum et librum Judicum et Ruth. David scripsit librum Psalmorum pro * decem senibus, scilicet pro homine primo, pro Melchisedece, pro Abrahamo, pro Mose, pro Hemano, pro Jeduthuno, pro

---

* According to Dr. Neubauer על ידי must be translated ".with the help of." If this translation be correct the tradition then signifies that each of the persons named possessed the same poetic and religious inspiration as David. Dalman (Marx) however (*Der Gottesname Adonaj*, p. 79 n.) defends the rendering of על ידי by "for, i. e. in the name of." See further Cheyne, *The Origin and Religious Contents of the Psalter*, London, 1891, p. 213.

Asapho et pro tribus Corae filliis. Jeremias scripsit librum suum et librum Regum et Threnos. Hiskias sociique ejus scripserunt Jesajam, Proverbia, Canticum Canticorum [et Ecclesiasten] *. Viri Synagogae magnae scripserunt Ezechielem et Duodecim, [Danielem] ** et libellum Esther. Ezra scripsit librum suum atque genealogias, quas Chronicorum in libro legimus, usque ad semet ipsum (עד לו)."

Thus far the Baraitha. We subjoin, for better understanding, the Gemara on the last words of the Baraitha: "Id cum Rabbi † effato convenit, quem Rabh Juda †† tradit dixisse: Ezra non ascendit e Babylonia, antequam suam genealogiam perscripsit; tum demum ascendit. — Quis ad finem perduxit? — Nehemias, filius Helchiae."

Although this tradition was not received into the Mishna, but as a Baraitha only into the Babylonian Talmud, it is not as recent as the latter. The Baraithas (Aramaic equivalent of משנה חיצונה), as appears from the formula by which they are quoted, תניא, were referred to the period of the Doctors of the Mishna (Tannaim). And this particular Baraitha is attributed to R. Judah I, surnamed ha-Kadosh, head of the school of Tiberias (2d century), to whom the collection of the Mishna is attributed. Let us examine its singular contents somewhat more closely. It strikes us immediately, that at the beginning of the tradition no mention is made of the Tora. This need not surprise us. For the Tora had always to be transcribed separately, never with other writings upon a single roll; and it is precisely for those who desire to copy the sacred books upon a single roll that rules are here given as to the

---

* [Omitted by Marx, p. 22, through an oversight.]
** [Omitted by Marx, p. 23.]
† [R. Abba Ariha; 3d century.]
†† [R. Juda ben Jehezkel; 3d century.]

sequence to be observed. Then follow the opinions about the
authorship of the several books. The Tora was written by Moses;
this was a matter of course. The ascription of the last eight
verses (about Moses' death) to Joshua is rational. Elsewhere in
the Talmud these eight *pesukim* also are attributed to Moses. In
Menahoth fol. 30a it is said: As far as ויֵמָת (Deut. 34, 5) the
Holy One, blessed be He, dictated and Moses repeated and wrote
down; from this ויֵמָת on He spoke and Moses wrote with
tears." But the ascription of the pericope about Balaam and
of Job to the great man of God is singular. Why is the pericope
Num. 22, 2—25, 9 a second time especially and expressly
ascribed to the author of the whole Pentateuch? This can, I
think, only be explained by the fact that doubts had arisen in
the Jewish schools (cf. Marx, *op. cit.* p. 42) concerning the
authorship of this strange story. That the book of Job is attributed to Moses is certainly connected with the theory that the
prophets wrote the history of their own times. Moses alone
wrote in addition the history of the old patriarchal times, and to
these times Job belonged. See, for an identification of Job with
Jobab (Gen. 36, 33) Marx, *op. cit.* p. 42, in connection with
the subscriprion to Job in the LXX translation. Not to mention
every point, we direct our attention in conclusion to the opinion
that Hezekiah and his assistants wrote the books designated by
the mnemonic symbol יִמְשֵׁ"ק (i. e. Isaiah, Proverbs, Canticles,
and Ecclesiastes), and the men of the Great Synagogue the
books קִנְדַ"ג (i. e. Ezekiel, Minor Prophets, Daniel, and The
Roll, i. e. Esther). It is often thought that this opinion is
connected with the later Jewish theory that sacred books could
only be written in the Holy Land. This would explain the assertion in regard to Ezekiel, Daniel and Esther. For this theory,
however, which originated with Rashi (Rabbi Shelomo ben Ishak,
† 1105), no ground is to be discovered in the Talmud (see Marx,
op. cit. p. 51). That the book תרי עשר (the Twelve Minor

§ 6. HISTORICAL EVIDENCE.

Prophets in one book) is attributed to the Men of the Great Synagogue, signifies only that this book as a whole must have had a single author (editor), distinct from the several prophets themselves. Malachi alone has a subscription, and thus the Twelve form together one book. Of the Men of the Great Synagogue we shall treat in particular in § 10. The four books which they are supposed to have written are in their present form all late except Ezekiel. Does there lurk here a dim reminiscence of the history of this book? We only raise the query; this is not the place to try to answer it. (See my *Letterkunde des Ouden Verbonds*, Groningen, 1893, § 15, n. 5.) The *voces memoriales* ימש״ק and קנד״ג are interpolated in the Hebrew text of the Baraitha and strangely formed. They correspond to the names קהלת, שיר השירים, משלי, ישעיה, and מגלת אסתר, דניאל, שנים עשר, יחזקאל, in the first case the four initial letters being taken, while in the second the letters ק, ג, ד, and ג are arbitrarily chosen.

Both in the Talmud and elsewhere various doubts of Jewish scholars are reported to us as to the canonical authority of some books of the Old Testament. Among these are opinions of teachers who lived in the second century of our era. But even in later post-Talmudic writings echoes of these doubts are still heard. They have to do chiefly with certain books of the Kethubim, Proverbs[4], Canticles, Ecclesiastes[5] and Esther[6]. In more than one place the authority of Ezekiel[7] is discussed, and in post-Talmudic writings judgments are reported about Jonah [8], which attract our attention.

[4] The passages which must be cited are as follows: On Proverbs, *Shabbath* fol. 30*b* and the post-Talmudic tract *Aboth de Rabbi Nathan*, c. i (an elaboration of the Talmudic treatise *Pirke Aboth*): on Canticles, *Yadaïm*, iii. 5 and *Aboth de Rabbi Nathan* c. i. on Ecclesiastes, *Eduyoth* v. 3, *Yadaïm* iii. 5, *Shabbath* fol. 30*ab*, *Aboth de Rabbi Nathan* c. i. *Leviticus Rabba* sec. 28 (7th century A. D.), *Midrash Koheleth* on ch. 1, 3 (7th century A. D.): on Esther, *Megilla* fol. 7*a*, *Jerus. Megilla* i. 4 (fol. 70), *Sanhedrin* fol. 100*a*: on Ezekiel, *Shabbath* fol. 13*b*, *Menahoth* fol. 45*a*, *Hagiga* fol. 13*a*: on Jonah only *Numeri Rabba* sec. 18 (12th century A. D.), and the Talmud commentary (falsely ascribed to Rashi) on *Taanith* fol. 15*a*.

In regard to Proverbs we read in *Shabbath* fol. 30*b*: "There was also an attempt to withdraw (לגנוז בקשו) the book of Proverbs, because it contained internal contradictions, but it was not withdrawn, because they [s. c. the learned] said, We have looked more deeply into Ecclesiastes and have found the solution; so we will in this case also investigate more deeply." In the context of the passage some contradictions are noted, together with some attempts at solution. — In *Aboth de Rabbi Nathan* c. 1 (cf. Zunz, *Die Gottesdienstlichen Vorträge der Juden*, p. 108 f, 2 ed., p. 114 f.) it is also said in regard to it: "At first it was said: Proverbs, Canticles, and Ecclesiastes are apocryphal, since they include parables (משלות), and thus do not belong to the sacred books; therefore they rose up and withdrew them, until the Men of the Great Synagogue came and explained them." While the memory of the doubts in regard to Proverbs is here still preserved, both the controversy over the canonicity of Proverbs (Cant. and Eccl.) and the decision are, in accordance with the later theory, transferred to remote antiquity.

5 In regard to the controversy over Canticles and Ecclesiastes, besides the passage just quoted from *Aboth de R. Nathan*, that from the Mishna *Yadaïm* iii. 5, is to be noted. It is evident from it that both Canticles and Ecclesiastes were regarded as canonical at the time of redaction of the Mishna (200 A. D), for this is taken for granted. But the controversy which had been carried on over this point had not yet been forgotten. We read: "All holy scriptures defile the hands. Canticles and Ecclesiastes defile the hands [i. e., are canonical; on the terminology see below, § 8, n. 2]. Rabbi Judah (ca. 120 A. D.) said, Canticles defiles the hands, but Ecclesiastes is subject of controversy. Rabbi Jose (contemporary of the emperor Hadrian) said, Ecclesiastes does not defile the hands, and Canticles is subject of controversy. Rabbi Simeon said, The school of Shammai was laxer as to Ecclesiastes than the school of Hillel (קהלת מקולי בית שמאי ומחומרי בית הלל; the school of Shammai did not regard Eccles. as canonical; that of Hillel did). Rabbi Simeon ben Azzai said. A tradition has been delivered to me from the lips of the seventy two elders, on the day when R. Eleazar ben Azariah was raised to the presidency (of the Academy), that Canticles and Ecclesiastes defile the hands. Rabbi Akiba [the well-known zealot for Barkokba] said: God forbid! No one in Israel ever contended that Canticles does not defile the hands! For the whole world together is not to be compared to the day on which Canticles was given to Israel; for all Kethubim are holy, but Canticles is most holy. If there was ever any controversy it was solely about Ecclesiastes. Rabbi Johanan ben Joshua, the son of R. Akiba's father-in-law, said: As [Simeon] ben Azzai reports, such was the controversy, and such was the decision."

With slight differences in details these statements occur in other places in the Talmud, e. g. in *Megilla* fol. 7*a*, where Simon ben Manasseh says that Canticles was inspired by the Holy Spirit, but that Ecclesiastes is a product of Solomon's own wisdom, and in *Eduyoth* v. 3. Of Ecclesiastes we read also in *Shabbath* fol. 30*b*: "The learned intended to withdraw the book Koheleth; but gave up the intention on account of the beginning and end of the book," שתחילתו דברי תורה וסופו דברי תורה; lit. "because its beginning consist of words of the Tora, and its end consists of words of the Tora," referring to 1, 3 and 12, 13. 14. The memory of doubts about Ecclesiastes has been preserved in later Midrashim also; *Levit. Rabba*, sec. 28 [Wünsche, p. 193]; *Koheleth Rabba* on ch. 1, 3 and 11, 9 [Wünsche, pp. 4, 150].

We observe, 1. that the controversy dates from a time as late as the beginning of the second century A. D. This is evident from the names of the rabbis mentioned as well as from the date, "the day on which Eleazar ben Azariah was raised to the presidency." This date occurs also elsewhere in the Talmud and must fall between 100 and 115 A. D. (Jost, *Gesch. d. Judenthums und seiner Sekten*, Leipzig, 1857, II. p. 25 ff.; Graetz, *Geschichte der Juden*, IV. Leipzig 1866, p. 37 ff.). 2. The declaration of Akiba, "All Kethubim are holy, but Canticles is most holy," shows us where we must look for the disputed books. The antilegomena of the Old Testament Canon must be sought in the third section. The doubts in regard to Ezekiel and Jonah are no exception to this; see below. 3. The emphatic language of the vehement fanatic and slavish literalist, Akiba, must not mislead us into thinking that there really had never been any doubts. For of Ecclesiastes he himself admits the fact, and the passionate protestation that Canticles is "most holy," would be entirely superfluous if this character had not been doubted.*

---

* [On Ecclesiastes see Schiffer, *Das Buch Kohelet nach der Auffassung der Weisen des Talmud u. Midrasch*, u. s. w., 1884; C. H. H. Wright.]

§ 6. HISTORICAL EVIDENCE

⁶ That the book of Esther, also, gave offence not only among Christians, but quite as much among Jews, is apparent from the passages adduced from the Babylonian Talmud. In the Babylonian Gemara of the tract *Megilla*, which treats of the reading of the "Roll" (i. e. Esther) and of the feast of Purim in general, we read as follows (fol. 7*a*) *: " R. Judah says [teaches]: Samuel taught that Esther does not defile the hands. Did Samuel then mean that Esther was not spoken by the Holy Spirit? Samuel undoubtedly taught that Esther was spoken by the Holy Spirit; but it was spoken to be recited and not to be written."

Manifestly the writer of these words is perplexed by the opinion of R. Samuel. He cannot deny that the latter taught that the book of Esther is not canonical. But that would never do! Samuel can not have meant that. It was even reported that he had said that Esther was spoken by the Holy Spirit. Accordingly his dictum could not possibly refer to the content; only the *written book* as such is meant.

It is quite possible that the second tradition in regard to Samuel, that Esther was indeed inspired by the Holy Spirit, is nothing more than a postulate of the author of this Gemara. To his mind, R. Samuel *could* not have denied this. And we must very probably credit the whole hair-splitting distinction, "inspired to be recited but not to be written," not to Samuel but to his reporter in the Gemara. There is thus a sound tradition that Rabbi Samuel taught that Esther does not defile the hands. (Against J. S. Bloch, *Studien*, u. s. w., p. 152 ff., cf. *infra*, § 8, n. 2).

In the Jerusalem Gemara, *Megilla* i. 4 (7) fol. 70 d. (Schwab, *Le Talmud de Jerusalem*, Paris, 1883, VI, p. 206 f.) it is reported by R. Samuel ben Naḥman on the authority of R. Jonathan,

---

* The canonicity of Canticles, Ecclesiastes and Ruth is also discussed, but we are here concerned with Esther only.

that eighty five elders, among whom were more than thirty prophets, were much put to it to legitimate the directions in Esther about the feast of Purim, in the face of the Pentateuch, of whose ordinances alone it is said that they were given by Yahwé to the children of Israel (Lev. 27, 34). They did not stir from the spot until God had enlightened their eyes and they read in Exod. 17, 14 that the Tora itself prescribes obedience to the directions of the book of Esther. This remarkable piece of exegesis should be read in Schwab, *l. c.* p. 207. — However unhistorical this account may be as a whole, it is evident that doubts are here preserved of the canonical authority of Esther, a fact which becomes of significance in conjunction with other accounts.

Finally we read in *Sanhedrin* fol. 100*a*, that Levi bar Samuel and Rabbi Huna bar Hiya were arranging covers [מטפחות, cases for the rolls] for the sacred books in the house of Rabbi Judah; "But when they came to the roll of Esther they said, this requires no covering. He said: this seems to be Epicureanism." Rashi indeed says on this passage that they could not have affirmed this, but must have asked the question (of Rabbi); but assuredly the man who spoke of Epicureanism believed that Esther did not defile the hands.

⁷ We can not be surprised that the book of Ezekiel has at all times presented to Jewish scholars many perplexing and difficult questions. "The beginning and the end of Ezekiel are involved in obscurity, and among the Hebrews these portions and the introduction of Genesis may not be read by any one who has not attained the age of thirty years." (Jerome *Epist. ad Paulinum, Ep.* 53, 8; *Opp.* ed. Vallarsi I. 277). In particular the conflict, which exists between the legal prescriptions of the last chapters (ch. 40—48) and the laws of the Pentateuch could not fail to excite attention. In *Menahoth* fol. 45*a* all the contradictions are enumerated and discussed, and the questioning

reader is referred to the remote future, when Elijah shall come and explain all these chapters. In *Shabbath* fol. 13*b* and *Hagiga* fol. 13*a* it is related (with various unimportant divergences) how the contradictions were resolved by Hananiah ben Hizkiah. This Hananiah prevented the book of Ezekiel from being withdrawn (גנזו) "because its words conflicted with those of the Tora. What, then, did he do? They brought him 300 jars of oil, and he sat in the upper chamber and explained it (or them, viz., the contradictions)."

The Hananiah ben Hizkiah (ben Garon) here named was a contemporary of Gamaliel I, the teacher of the apostle Paul. According to Fürst (*Kanon*, p. 24) he was a younger contemporary of Hillel and lived about the time of the birth of Christ. Graetz (*Geschichte der Juden*, III. p. 499) thinks that Eleazar, the son of Hananiah, should have been named instead of his father, and fixes the decision of the controversy about Ezekiel in 66 A. D.

We must observe, 1. that these accounts do not occur in the Mishna, like those concerning Canticles and Ecclesiastes, but in the Gemara. 2. That the decision is put before 50 A. D.; a century earlier, therefore, than that about Canticles and Ecclesiastes. 3. That no names are given of scribes who would have "withdrawn" Ezekiel, as there are in the case of Eccl., Cant. and Esther. This leads us to infer that Ezekiel was originally regarded as sacred; the contradictions were indeed noticed, but faith took it for granted that a prophet like Elijah both could, and some day would, explain them. A later doctor of the law deemed that the conflict with the Pentateuch might well have led to Ezekiel's being "withdrawn"; that this did not come to pass, he attributed to the laborious efforts of Hananiah ben Hizkiah, whose explanations doubtless smelled of the lamp. When it was once accepted that there was no conflict between Ezekiel and the Tora some went so far as to quote from this prophet as "from the Tora" (*Moed Katan* fol. 5*a*); and in accordance with the notion of the oral law (cf. § 9 n. 8) it was taught that the ordinances of Ezekiel also had been handed down by tradition from Moses, and that Ezekiel had only reduced them to writing (Fürst, *Kanon*, p. 53). We have no report of any formal controversy in which a scribe in so many words declared Ezekiel apocryphal. The antilegomena of the O. T. are thus to be sought in the third section alone.

I must still maintain this view against Buhl, who contends (*Kanon*, p. 30 [mistranslated *Canon and Text*, p. 30]) that the doubts in regard to Ezekiel are of the same nature as those in regard to some of the Kethubim. This is connected with Buhl's theory that all the doubts reported in Jewish sources affect a Canon already definitely fixed, and can have in view nothing more than a revision of this (see Buhl, *l. c.* p. 27, Eng. trans. p. 27 f., and cf. below § 11, n. 9). But, as will appear later, it is impossible to point to any official decision of the school on the canonicity of Esther, the Prophets or the Kethubim before the second century A. D. All that actually existed in the lifetime of Hananiah, in the case of the Prophets as well as of the Kethubim, was a *communis opinio*; but in the case of the former, this opinion had, in the two centuries that the collection had existed, become unalterable. The Kethubim could at that time not yet boast of such authority. Finally, it is to be observed that in the case of Ezekiel (and Proverbs) there is only talk of "withdrawing" the book, and it is not said that it does not "defile the hands." König (*Einleitung in das A. T.*, p. 453) draws from this the inference that the discussion about these two books had to do not with their canonicity, but with their use in the synagogue, — two things which according to him must not be confounded, as they are at least not entirely equivalent. As only men above thirty years of age were allowed to read [the beginning and end of] Ezekiel, the question might very well be raised, quite independently of that of the canonicity, whether it was not desirable that books which seemed to be in conflict with the Tora, like Ezekiel, or self contradictory, like Proverbs, should be excluded from the readings in the Synagogue. To us it seems that the difference in the form in which the objections are reported is accidental; at least R. Nathan (see n. 4) apparently did not make this distinction. Moreover, we shall show in § 8 that the question of canonicity virtually coincides with the question whether a book is allowed to be read in the synagogue or not; cf. § 8 n. 2, and the application which Jerome makes of the word *ganaz* (§ 8, n. 2).

8 The passages cited about Jonah do not contradict this view. Moreover, they are chiefly opinions of the 12th century A. D., or later. For completeness' sake we will briefly mention their contents. *Numeri Rabba*, sec. 18 (Warsaw ed. fol. יט *a*; Wünsche, p. 451), in connection with plays upon the numbers 50, 60 and 80 in Is. 3, 3 and Cant. 6, 8, which are combined with sacred things, we read; "*Captain of fifty* (Is. 3, 3): The Twenty Four (sacred books), plus eleven of the Twelve (Minor Prophets) — excluding Jonah because it is (a book) by itself — and the Six Sedarim (of the Mishna), and the nine sections of Torath Kohanim (Halachic work on Leviticus) make together fifty."

As regards the exception made of the book of Jonah, we get light from the commentary *Matnoth Kehunna* (a work of the 16th century) on this passage. After giving the list of the 24 books, the author notes that Jonah is counted separately because it is exclusively occupied with the heathen and Israel is not mentioned in it, as Radak (R. David Kimchi, † 1240) writes in the introduction to his commentary on the book of Jonah. This passage, accordingly, only teaches us that the Jews of the middle ages raised the question, How came Jonah, which does not treat of Israel, to be inserted among Israel's sacred writings?

That its canonicity was doubted in earlier times there is no evidence.

The case is somewhat different with the remarks of the commentator ("Pseudo-Rashi") on *Taanith* fol. 15*a*, since they are based on a distinction made in the Mishna itself. The passage in the Mishna reads as follows (*Taanith* ii. 1): "Of the men of Niniveh it is not said, And God saw their sackcloth and their fasting; but (Jonah 3, 10), And God saw their works, that they turned again from their evil way. And in the Kabbala he says, Rend your hearts and not your garments (Joel 2, 13)." It is unmistakable that the two passages from Jonah and Joel are not cited in the same way. Joel's words are esteemed to belong to the Kabbala (tradition), and this is said in a way which suggests that the words from Jonah 3, 10 were not so regarded. This difference attracted the attention of the commentator, who remarks on the words ובקבלה הוא אומר (and in the Kabbala He saith, — the usual formula of quotation) that the quotation from Joel is called Kabbala, while that from Jonah is not, because "all passages in which the prophet commands, instructs, and warns Israel are called *Kabbala;* but the passages which are not commanded to a prophet, like this, 'and God saw' &c, in which he relates a fact and proceeds to draw a lesson from it incidentally, are not called *Kabbala*." If we had here to do only with a hair-splitting distinction of a mediæval Jewish rabbi, we might leave the matter here. But this is not the case. The commentator's note is an explanation of a passage in the Mishna, and an explanation which must be pronounced in the main correct. There is no intimation of any doubt about the canonical authority of the prophetic book of Jonah. But it does follow from this passage of the Mishna, as we shall show more fully in a later paragraph, that from the Jewish point of view the Prophets, in contrast to the Law, are *tradition;* and that they thus really possess authority only in so far as their admonitions may be regarded as further explaining and applying the commandments and prohibitions of the Law. It is obvious that from this point of view the book of Jonah occupies an unique position among the prophets. It is really surprising that no tradition reports that any Tannaim (teachers of the Mishna) questioned its canonicity. This can only be explained by the fact that in the first century A. D. the second division was already regarded as long since established, and that in Jonah no such conflict with the law was discovered as in Ezekiel.

Summing up the results of our enquiry in this paragraph we must draw the following conclusions: 1. The Talmudic accounts, taken as a whole, are decidedly opposed to the opinion adopted from Elias Levita that the canonization of the Old Testament was already consummated by Ezra in the 5th century B. C.[9]. 2. The Mishna already presupposes our Canon in its threefold division. In the year 200 A. D. the matter was therefore settled; the final decision of the schools cannot, however, at that time have been much more than a half-century old. Down into the second century of our era the canonical authority of Proverbs, Ecclesiastes, Canticles, and Esther was warmly debated by Jewish scholars [10].

[9] All the evidence collected in the preceding paragraph fully establishes the position taken in the text. Such warm discussions about some books of the third division are quite inexplicable

if we must assume that the Canon had been fixed before the year 400 B. C., and by a man of Ezra's authority. To this it must be added that the Talmud, which extols the work of Ezra so highly as to declare that "Ezra would have been worthy that the Tora should have been given to Israel by his hand, if Moses had not preceded him," (*Babyl. Sanhedrin c.* i. [fol. 21*b* end]; *Jerus. Megilla c.* i. 8 (11) fol. 71*b* end; see the excellent translation of M. Schwab, *Le Talmud de Jerusalem*, Paris, 1883, VI. p. 212), nowhere in unambiguous words ascribes to Ezra the work of canonization. The passage *Baba Bathra* fol. 15 treats of the editing of certain books, but not of their canonization; though in the mind of later Jewish writers the two ideas run into one.

An inclination is indeed perceptible in the Talmud to refer the redaction of *all* the books (as in 4 (2) Esdras) to Ezra's days. This is also the intention of the accounts which ascribe this work to Ezra in conjunction with the Men of the Great Synagogue. It was formerly erroneously thought that these statements preserved a reminiscence of the part which the scribes after Ezra had in the work (see §. 10, n. 12). But although in the Talmud itself a tendency is manifest which later Jewish scholars developed into a settled opinion, taken as a whole the Talmudic accounts are opposed to this idea.

[10] When all the evidence which we have adduced from the Talmud is duly considered, it will have to be admitted that the conclusion drawn in the text is legitimate. It will be observed that we make no mention of the doubts about Ezekiel and Jonah. There is no sufficient reason for believing that any Jewish scholar ever wished to remove either of these prophets from the second division. Fürst (*Kanon*, p. 95) in my opinion, therefore, goes too far when he writes: "It was this Hananiah too who harmonized the contradictions between Ezekiel and the Tora, and so made possible the reception of Ezekiel into the

Canon." In 32 B. C., the year in which Fürst places this decision, the collection of the Nebiim had doubtless long been regarded as closed. Why else was the book of Daniel not admitted to it? In this collection Ezekiel was certainly included. Was an attempt made to remove this book from the second division? We are not told the name of any Rabbi who ventured this bold move. In spite of the conflict with the Tora, the book was evidently regarded as sacred because of the authority of the prophet; leaving it to Elijah, who was to come, to explain how this was possible in the face of the Tora. At a later time Hananiah attempted the solution himself, and thus prevented the possibility that any one should ever "withdraw" Ezekiel.— Nor was Jonah ever a subject of controversy. At a very late period, however, it was thought strange that this book, containing no message to Israel, should stand beside the other prophets; and even at an earlier time (*Taanith* ii. 1 [fol. 15*a*]) its contents were not regarded as *Kabbala*. But by the same rule by far greater part of the *prophetae priores* is not Kabbala either. And no trace of doubt about the canonical authority of these books is to be discovered anywhere.

The result therefore remains, that in the second century A. D. there was still vigorous dispute about some books of the Kethubim, viz. Proverbs, Ecclesiastes, Canticles, and Esther.—It is not legitimate to try to weaken the significance of the passages quoted from the Mishna and Gemara as Strack does in his article "Kanon des A. T." (*P.R.E*^{2}., VII. p. 429) by the remark, that these discussions often make the impression that the difficulties are raised only to be refuted, for the sake of proving that the authority of the books was assured, or of exercising the acuteness of the disputants. This is more or less true of what has been quoted about Ezekiel; but the discussions in regard to Ecclesiastes and Canticles, for example, are as far as possible from making this impression. The reader may judge for himself. But beside this, the passion with which Akiba declares Canticles to be "most holy," and with which another Rabbi, Simeon ben Lakish (about 300 A. D.; see Fürst, *Kanon*, p. 70) puts Esther on an equality with the Tora and above the Prophets and the Hagiographa, make it very evident that there were men in Israel who deemed that these books were not altogether in place in the series of Sacred Scriptures in which they were put by the majority of the scribes. Talmudic and other passages from which it appears that scribes of the first century before and after Christ quoted Ecclesiastes as canonical may be found in Cheyne, *Job and Solomon, or the Wisdom of the O. T.*, London, 1887, p. 280. But over against this the fact should be noted that the author of the Wisdom of Solomon in 2, 1—9 manifestly directs a polemic against this book; cf. Buhl, *Kanon*, p. 23, Engl. Transl. p. 23.

§ 7.

HISTORICAL EVIDENCE CONCERNING THE CANON OF THE OLD TESTAMENT, CONTINUED.

e. THE CHRISTIAN CHURCH FATHERS.

Not all the passages in the Church Fathers which expressly or indirectly give information concerning the Old Testament Canon require to be taken into account as evidence bearing on the history of the Canon. For our enquiry only those statements of the Fathers are of any value which they make as the result of their own investigations in Jewish circles. From the Eastern Church we have the Canon of Melito, Bishop of Sardis (died after 171 A. D.), which omits the book of Esther, probably not by accident [1]; and the Canon of Origen (died 254 A. D.), which names Esther last and includes Baruch [2].

[1] The Canon of Melito of Sardis is preserved to us by Eusebius in his *Hist. Eccl.* iv. 26 [Ed. Heinichen, 1868, p. 195]. It is important for us because Melito says that he made a journey to the East in order carefully to investigate, on the very spot where the words of the O. T. had been published and the events had taken place, what was the number and order of the books (πόσα τὸν ἀριθμὸν καὶ ὁποῖα τὴν τάξιν εἶεν). As the result of this investigation he sends to Onesimus, the brother, the following list: Μωϋσέως πέντε. Γένεσις, Ἔξοδος, Λευιτικόν, Ἀριθμοί *, Δευτερονόμιον· Ἰησοῦς Ναυῆ, Κριταί, Ροὶθ· Βασιλειῶν τέσσαρα, Παραλειπομένων δίο. Ψαλμῶν Δαβιδ, Σαλομῶνος Παροιμίαι, ἡ καὶ Σοφία, Ἐκκλησιαστής, ⁵Ἀσμα Ἀσμάτων, Ἰώβ. Προφητῶν, Ἡσαΐου, Ἱερεμίου, τῶν δώδεκα ἐν μονοβίβλῳ, Δανιήλ, Ἰεζεκιήλ, Ἔσδρας. (The whole passage is printed in de Wette's *Lehrbuch der Hist.-krit. Einleitung*, edited by Dr. Eb. Schrader, 8 ed. 1869, p. 52). The order is certainly strange, and agrees neither with the Alexandrian nor with the Palestinian enumeration. Whether it is to be attributed to Melito's informant or to the bishop himself may be left undecided. That Nehemiah and Lamentations are wanting need occasion no surprise. They are counted in with Ezra and

---

* [The manuscript authority strongly support the order, Ἀριθμοι, Λευιτικόν; see Heinichen.]

Jeremiah respectively. But the fact that Esther is missing is noteworthy. We cannot suppose that it is included in Ezra-Nehemiah; and to assert that it has been omitted by copyists is much too easy a solution. Nor will it do to suppose that Melito showed his Jewish informant the Greek book of Esther from the LXX, and that the Jew declared this apocryphal. For then it would have been natural for Melito to accept a shorter redaction of Esther. If the fact were isolated we should perhaps have to look about us for some such explanation. We know, however, that doubts of the canonicity of Esther were really entertained in authoritative Jewish circles (see § 6, n. 6); that Origen (see this § n. 2) names Esther last; and that in the 4th. century Athanasius (*Epist. festalis* of the year 365, *Opp.* ed. Bened. I. 961) and Gregory Nazianzen (died 389; *Carm.* xxxiii, *Opp.* II. 98, ed. Colon.) regard this book as uncanonical. In this state of the case we must consider, I think, that the omission is intentional, and probably due to the opinion of Melito's Jewish informant. The feast of Purim, which was kept in the remote East, could not get a firm footing in Palestine. The fast upon the 13th of Adar, in accordance with Esther 9, 31, was for centuries not observed there, because this day was a joyful anniversary of the victory of Judas the Maccabee over Nicanor (1 Macc. 7, 48; cf. W. Robertson Smith, *O. T. in the Jewish Church*, 2 ed. 1892, p. 183.) And it is no wonder that the Christians did not at once receive into the number of their Sacred Scriptures this book, which passed among the Jews themselves as doubtful. It seems to have been pretty generally rejected. As an exception we read in the *Iambi ad Seleucum* of Amphilochius, Bp. of Iconium († 395) [inter *Opp. Greg. Naz.*, ed. Colon. 1680, II. 194 f.; Migne, *Patrologia Graeca*, XXXVII. 1593 f.], "With these some count in Esther also (τούτοις προσεγκρίνουσι τὴν Ἐσθὴρ τινές). Esther is included among the canonical books in canon 60 of the Council of Laodicea; in the *Apostolic Canons*, can. 85

(*Const. Apost.* ed. Ueltzen, p. 253; in Cyril of Jerusalem [*Catech.* iv. 35] and in Epiphanius. See de Wette-Schrader, *Einl.*, p. 56, 57).

² The Canon of Origen also is preserved to us by Eusebius (*Hist. eccl.* vi. 25). Manifestly the account of this learned Church-father, who for the text of the O. T. too seeks after the "Hebrew verity," rests upon a knowledge of the original which he can only have acquired from the Jews. He informs us that the number of books is 22, corresponding to the number of the letters of the alphabet (δύο καὶ εἴκοσι ὅσος ἀριθμὸς τῶν παρ' αὐτοῖς στοιχείων ἐστίν). The list, giving the Greek and Hebrew names with an interpretation of the latter, is as follows: Εἰσὶ δὲ αἱ εἴκοσι δύο βίβλοι καθ' Ἑβραίους αἵδε· ἡ παρ' ἡμῖν Γένεσις ἐπιγεγραμμένη, παρ' Ἑβραίοις δὲ ἀπὸ τῆς ἀρχῆς τῆς βίβλου Βρησὶδ, ὅπερ ἐστίν, ἐν ἀρχῇ· Ἔξοδος, Οὐελεσμώθ, ὅπερ ἐστί, ταῦτα τὰ ὀνόματα· Λευιτικόν, Οὐϊκρά, καὶ ἐκάλεσεν· Ἀριθμοί, Ἀμμεσφεκωδείμ· Δευτερονόμιον, Ἐλεαδδεβαρείμ, οὗτοι οἱ λόγοι· Ἰησοῦς υἱὸς Ναυῆ, Ἰωσοῦε βὲν Νοῦν· Κριταί, Ῥούθ, παρ' αὐτοῖς ἐν ἑνί, Σωφατείμ· Βασιλειῶν πρώτη, δευτέρα, παρ' αὐτοῖς ἕν, Σαμουήλ, ὁ θεόκωητος· Βασιλειῶν τρίτη, τετάρτη, ἐν ἑνὶ Οὐαμμέλεχ Δαβίδ, ὅπερ ἐστί, βασιλεία Δαβίδ· Παραλειπομένων πρώτη, δευτέρα, ἐν ἑνὶ Δαβρηϊαμείν, ὅπερ ἐστί, λόγοι ἡμερῶν· Ἔσδρας πρῶτος, δεύτερος, ἐν ἑνὶ Ἐζρά, ὅ ἐστι, βοηθός· Βίβλος Ψαλμῶν, Σφαρθελλείμ· Σολομῶντος Παροιμίαι, Μισλώθ· Ἐκκλησιατής, Κωέλεθ· Ἆσμα Ἀισμάτων (οὐ γὰρ ὡς ὑπολαμβάνουσί τινες, Ἄσματα Ἀσμάτων), Σὶρ Ἀσσιρίμ· Ἡσαΐας, Ἰεσσία· Ἱερεμίας σὺν Θρήνοις καὶ τῇ ἐπιστολῇ ἐν ἑνί, Ἰερεμία· Δανιήλ, Δανιήλ· Ἰεζεκιήλ, Ἰεζικήλ· Ἰώβ, Ἰώβ· Ἐσθήρ, Ἐσθήρ. Ἔξω δὲ τούτων ἐστὶ τὰ Μακκαβαϊκά, ἅπερ ἐπιγέγραπται Σαρβὴθ Σαρβανιέλ.

Several points here require our attention. First of all we observe that the Twelve Minor prophets are wanting. This, it need hardly be said, is not intentional; the omission has occurred either through an inadvertence of Eusebius, or through that of the copyist. For Origen announces 22 books and enu-

merates only 21. Moreover, in the Latin translation of Rufinus *
the *Dodekapropheton* appears immediately following Canticles
(cf. de Wette-Schrader, *Einleitung*, p. 53). In the next place,
we find Esther named last, and we have already learned what
this signifies. But Origen also adds something to the list. For
he not only attaches Lamentations to Jeremiah, but connects
with it ἡ ἐπιστολή also. Under this name Baruch too is certainly included. The question is, Does Origen here really repeat
what his Jewish informants had told him; or does he add Baruch
merely from his own familiarity with the Greek Bible? The
latter is not impossible. In his enquiry Origen took the LXX
as his starting point, and brought the Jewish accounts as far as
he could into harmony with it; a course which he pursued also in
his laborious work on the text of the O. T. But to return to
Baruch. It is not impossible that Origen had a Jewish informant
who saw no objection to reckoning the book of Baruch as a
part of Jeremiah; if, at least, it be true, as the *Apostolic Consti-
tutions* report, that the Jews in the third century A. D., on the
Great Day of Atonement read Baruch as well as Lamentations
in the synagogue. (*Const. apost.* v. 20; ed. Ueltzen p. 124.) But
this statement, which is quite unsupported, cannot be unhesitatingly
accepted. The author is a polemical zealot; and moreover the
further question arises, Among what Jews did this custom exist?
It may possibly have been done in a synagogue here and there,
but in authoritative circles Baruch was not recognized. —
The word Ἀμμεσφεκοδείμ as a Hebrew name for Ἀριθμοί is a
transcription of חוֹמֶשׁ פְּקוּדִים **.

---

* [Origen, *Opp.* ed. Delarue II. 529.]

** [Book of Musters (lit. Fifth Part, *sc.* of the Pentateuch, of the Mustered
Men); the name is derived from the formula in which the total fighting
strength of each tribe is given, Num 1, 21. 23., &c. — "All the mustered
men (כל פקדיהם) of the tribe of .... were .... thousand," &c.]

In Latin Christendom it is Jerome (died 420) who tells us what he had learned from his Jewish teachers. In the famous *Prologus galeatus* he gives us light on the subject of the Canon of the Old Testament as a whole [3]; and in his commentary on Ecclesiastes he shows that he is acquainted with the doubts of Jewish scholars in regard to that book [4].

[3] Jerome began his celebrated version of the Bible in the year 385 at Bethlehem, with the help of Jewish scholars (see *Praef. in Job.*). In 390 the first part of it was published, the translation of the books of Samuel and Kings. For this reason the translation of these books is preceded by so extended a preface. "Hic prologus Scripturarum" — he writes at the conclusion of the preface — "quasi galeatum principium omnibus libris, quos de Hebraeo vertimus in Latinum, convenire potest." Hence the name *Prologus galeatus* ordinarily given to this *Praefatio Regnorum*. The passage as a whole reads as follows (de Wette-Schrader, *Einleitung*, p. 61 ; Bleek-Wellhausen, *Einleitung* [4], 1878, p. 548 ff.) *: "Viginti et duas litteras esse apud Hebraeos Syrorum quoque et Chaldaeorum lingua testatur, quae Hebraeae magna ex parte confinis est, nam et ipsi viginti duo elementa habent eodem sono sed diversis characteribus. Samaritani etiam Pentateuchum Mosi totidem litteris scriptitant, figuris tantum et apicibus discrepantes. Certumque est Ezram scribam legisque doctorem post capta Hierosolyma et instaurationem

* [*Opp.* ed. Vallarsi, IX, 453 ff.; the Preface may also be found in any authorized edition of the Vulgate — not in the mutilated Latin Bibles issued by the Bible Societies.]

templi sub Zorobabel alias litteras reperisse quibus nunc utimur, cum ad illud usque tempus iidem Samaritanorum et Hebraeorum characteres fuerint. In libro quoque Numerorum haec eadem supputatio, sub levitarum ac sacerdotum censu, mystice ostenditur. Et nomen Domini tetragrammaton in quibusdam graecis voluminibus usque hodie antiquis expressum litteris invenimus. Sed et Psalmi xxxvi et cx et cxi et cxviii et cxxxxiv quanquam diverso scribantur metro tamen ejusdem numeri texuntur alphabeto. Et Hieremiae Lamentationes et oratio eius, Salomonis quoque in fine Proverbia ab eo loco in quo ait: Mulierem fortem quis inveniet—iisdem alphabetis vel incisionibus supputantur. Porro quinque litterae duplices apud eos sunt, *caph mem nun pe sade:* aliter enim per has scribunt principia medietatesque verborum, aliter fines. Unde et quinque a plerisque libri duplices aestimantur, Samuhel, Malachim, Dabre-iamin, Ezras, Hieremias cum Cinoth, i. e. Lamentationibus suis. Quomodo igitur viginti duo elementa sunt per quae scribimus Hebraice omne quod loquimur, et eorum initiis vox humana comprehenditur, ita viginti duo volumina supputantur quibus, quasi litteris et exordiis in Dei doctrina, tenera adhuc et lactans viri iusti eruditur infantia. Primus apud eos liber vocatur *Bresith*, quem nos Genesim dicimus. Secundus *Hellesmoth*, qui Exodus appellatur. Tertius *Vaiecra* i. e. Leviticus. Quartus *Vaiedabber*, quem Numeros vocamus. Quintus *Addabarim*, qui Deuteronomium praenotatur. Hi sunt quinque libri Mosi quos proprie *Thorath* i. e. Legem appellant. Secundum *Prophetarum* ordinem faciunt et incipiunt ab Hiesu filio Nave, qui apud eos *Josue ben Nun* dicitur. Deinde subtexunt *Sophtim* i. e. Iudicum librum, et in eundem compingunt *Ruth* quia in diebus iudicum facta narratur historia. Tertius sequitur *Samuhel*, quem nos Regnorum primum et secundum dicimus. Quartus *Malachim* i. e. Regum, qui tertio et quarto Regnorum volumine continetur; meliusque multo est *Malachim* i. e. regum quam Malachoth

i. e. regnorum dicere, non enim multa gentium regna describit sed unius Israelitici populi qui tribubus duodecim continetur. Quintus *Esaias*. Sextus *Hieremias*. Septimus *Hiezecihel*. Octavus liber Duodecim Prophetarum, qui apud illos vocatur *Thare-asar*. Tertius ordo *Hagiographa* possidet. Et primus liber incipit a *Job*. Secundus a *David*, quem quinque incisionibus et uno Psalmorum volumine comprehendunt. Tertius est *Solomon* tres libros habens: Proverbia quae illi parabolas i. e. *Masaloth* appellant et Ecclesiasten i. e. *Accoeleth* et Canticum Canticorum quem titulo *Sir-assirim* praenotant. Sextus est Danihel. Septimus *Dabre-iamin* i. e. verba dierum, quod signigicantius chronicon totius divinae historiae possumus appellare; qui liber apud nos Paralipomenon primus et secundus inscribitur. Octavus *Ezras*, qui et ipse similiter apud Graecos et Latinos in duos libros divisus est. Nonus *Esther*. Atque ita fiunt pariter veteris legis libri viginti duo i. e. *Mosi* quinque, *Prophetarum* octo, *Hagiographorum* novem. Quanquam nonnulli Ruth et Cinoth inter Hagiographa scriptitent et libros hos in suo putent numero supputandos, ac per hoc esse priscae legis libros vigintiquatuor; quos sub numero vigintiquatuor seniorum Apocalypsis Johannis [Cap. 4, 4 seq.] inducit adorantes agnum et coronas suas prostratis vultibus offerentes—stantibus coram quatuor animalibus oculatis et retro et ante, i. e. in praeteritum et in futurum respicientibus et indefessa voce clamantibus: sanctus sanctus sanctus, Dominus Deus omnipotens, qui erat et qui est et qui futurus est. Hic prologus Scripturarum quasi galeatum principium omnibus libris, quos de Hebraeo vertimus in Latinum, convenire potest, ut scire valeamus quicquid extra hos est inter apocrypha seponendum. Igitur Sapientia quae vulgo Solomonis inscribitur et Hiesu filii Sirach liber et Judith et Tobias et Pastor non sunt in canone. Machabaeorum primum librum Hebraeicum reperi, secundus Graecus est, quod ex ipsa quoque phrasi probari potest," etc.

What Jerome tells us about the Hebrew characters serves chiefly to explain the number 22, and to illustrate the fact, that, as there are five double letters (because of the final letters ךםןףץ), so there are five double books, viz. Samuel, Kings, Chronicles, Ezra-Nehemiah, and Jeremiah-Lamentations. On the whole he faithfully reproduces the Palestinian principle of the three-fold division of the Canon; he departs from it only in the order of the books, and Esther is again named last. The number 24, also, is not unknown to Jerome. "Some include Ruth and Lamentations among the Hagiographa and count these books separately." If we should give these words their full weight, it would follow that the familiar arrangement of our own Hebrew Bibles originated in Jerome's time. So Kuenen, *H. K. O*[1]. III p. 450, n. 8; cf. above § 1, n. 12. That it was only *some* (nonnulli) who preferred to count in this way, Jerome no doubt learned from the same source from which he got the notion that the Apocalypse of John introduces these twenty four books "sub numero vigintiquatuor seniorum adorantes agnum et coronas suas prostratis vultibus offerentes." The only inference to be drawn from this passage, in my opinion, is that the usual enumeration of twenty four was not unknown to him; or at most, that he got his information from a Jew who himself was somewhat under Alexandrian influence. At a later time he was more correctly informed ([*Praef. in Danielem*] cf. § 11, n. 2). But that it first originated in Jerome's days is contradicted, among other things, by the testimony of the Baraitha in *Baba Bathra* fol. 14*b*, 15*a*; see § 6, n. 3; § 11, n. 2. the Wisdom of Solomon, Jesus Sirach, Judith, Tobit, the Shepherd of Hermas, and Maccabees, — even 1 Macc., which he knew in the Hebrew — he classes among the apocrypha. Other statements, such as those in *Epist.* 53. *ad Paulinum* (*Opp.* ed. Vallarsi, I 268 ff. [§ 8, col. 274—277], see Kuenen, *H. K. O*[1]. III. p. 418) must be given a secondary place, as less exact than the detailed account of the *Prologus galeatus*.

4 See the Commentary on Ecclesiastes, 12, 13. 14. (*Opp.* ed. Vallarsi, III. 496). "Aiunt Hebraei, quum inter cetera scripta Solomonis quae antiquata sunt nec in memoria duraverunt et hic liber oblitterandus videretur, eo quod vanas Dei assereret creaturas et totum putaret esse pro nihilo, et cibum et potum et delicias transeuntes praeferret omnibus, ex hoc uno capitulo meruisse auctoritatem ut in divinorum voluminum numero poneretur, quod totam disputationem suam et omnem catalogum hac quasi ἀνακεφαλαιώσει coarctaverit et dixerit finem sermonum suorum auditu esse promptissimum nec aliquid in se habere difficile, ut scilicet Deum timeamus et eius praecepta faciamus." On account of its contents, therefore, Ecclesiastes would not have been received; but on account of the outcome at the end of the book it was considered worthy to be included "in divinorum voluminum numero". This agrees substantially with the statements in the Talmud, *Shabbath* fol. 30 *a.b* (cf. § 6, n. 5).

The result of our enquiry in this paragraph is that according to the Church Fathers also the book of Esther was not universally recognized in Jewish circles; and that the doubts in regard to Ecclesiastes were known to Christian scholars such as Jerome [5].

5 The statement in the text has been sufficiently demonstrated. Were we writing a history of the O. T. Canon in the Christian church, we should further show how little permanent influence

the enquiries which Christian scholars made of the Jews exerted. Origen himself is inconsistent (see de Wette-Schrader, *Einleitung, p.* 53, *c*). On the whole, however, they were stricter in the East. Hence the Synod of Laodicea (between 360 and 370) rejected the apocrypha of the O. T.; while those of Hippo and Carthage (393, 397) admitted the validity of the apocrypha to corroborate the dogma of the church (cf. our Introductory Remarks, and Prof. J. Cramer, *De Kanon der H. S. in de eerste Vier Eeuwen*, Amsterdam, 1883, p. 49). It is also noteworthy that the Nestorian Christians do not acknowledge the canonical authority of Esther nor of the writings of the Chronicler (Chronicles, Ezra-Nehemiah); see Nöldeke in *Zeitschrift der Deutschen Morgenl. Gesellschaft*, XXXII, 1878, p. 587; XXXV, 1881, p. 496. In the national Bible of the Syrians, the Peshito, the book of Chronicles was originally wanting, and only at a later time was a Jewish targum of this book incorporated in it, without, however, securing universal recognition. The Nestorian canon is probably based upon the teaching of Theodore of Mopsuestia, who disputed the canonical authority of Chronicles, Ezra-Nehemiah, Esther, and even of Job.* It is remarkable that the Nestorians, while they thus abbreviated the Canon, nevertheless accepted as canonical Jesus ben Sirach and the apocryphal additions to Daniel, against the mind of the council of Laodicea (cf. Buhl, *Kanon u. Text d. A. T.*, p. 52 ; Engl. transl. p. 53 f.

---

* [See Kihn, *Theodor von Mopsuestia und Junilius Africanus als Exegeten*, 1880, p. 65, 67 f.]

§ 8.

THE IDEA OF CANONICITY IN THE JEWISH SCHOOLS.

Having examined the various historical evidences, it remains to sketch in outline the history of the canonization of the Old Testament books. We shall strive to form a conception of the course of events which shall accord with the results we have reached by the way of historical criticism; and shall especially endeavour to apprehend the inner significance of the historical process. To do this, it is necessary at the outset to know what significance the Jews attached to the setting of their Sacred Scriptures in a class by themselves.

The Jewish notions on this point are not equivalent to our concept *canonical*[1]. The discussions upon the question whether certain Scriptures should not be "withdrawn, hid away" show us that the real question was whether a given book was or not suitable for public reading at the religious exercises of the synagogue[2]; and the same thing is perhaps implied in the expression, "Holy Scriptures defile the hands."

---

[1] Wellhausen rightly observes (*Einleitung*[4], p. 547, n. 1.) "Kanon ist ein kirchlicher Terminus, von den griechischen

Vätern im vierten Jahrh. für diejenigen Bücher aufgebracht, welche in die Sammlung der heiligen Classiker ἐγκρίνονται." * Now this ecclesiastical term has no equivalent in the Jewish schools, unless we retain the more formal definition of the word canon which Semler proposed (*Abhandlung von freier Untersuchung des Canon*, I. 14, Th. II, Vorrede). He held that κανών meant only a list of books which might be read in the church. Since K. A. Credner, however (*Zur Geschichte des Kanons*, 1847), the material sense has been made more prominent; and it has been thought that the meaning 'rule, plumbline, standard,' which the word has in classical Greek would naturally be applied to the Sacred Scriptures, in which was sought the κανών τῆς ἀληθείας καὶ τῆς πίστεως.

There is an element of truth in the views of both Semler and Credner. This is not the place to show this in detail; I will indicate but one point; Semler is right in his opinion that the original significance of *canon* was purely formal, and maintaining that the meaning, standard, norm of faith and practise, was not thought of; γραφαὶ κανονιζόμεναι were originally the same as what were anciently called ὁμολογούμενα. But in this purely formal definition we leave out of view the fact that there was a reason for making books canonical. This reason lay in the recognition of the sacred, theopneustic character of the Scriptures. Hence it was, that, when once this appellation had come into general use, the signification of standard or norm of faith and practise was given to it. This was natural. Before the name canonical had displaced the older name ὁμολογούμενα, κανών ἐκκλησιαστικός (or τῆς πίστεως) meant the *regula fidei*, the epitome of what passed as Christian and churchly teaching.

---

* ["Canon is an ecclesiastical term, brought into use by the Greek Fathers in the 4th century for those books which were received (ἐγκρίνονται) into the collection of sacred classics."]

§ 8. THE IDEA OF CANONICITY

As its source, certain writings (even extra-Biblical ones) are noted as of normative authority; and in this sense Origen, for instance, already speaks (in Rufinus's translation) of *scripturae canonicae*.* In the Christian church "canonical" thus acquired a material sense which has no equivalent in the Jewish schools.

It is needless to say that the Jewish theologians applied a material standard in determining what books might or might not be read in the synagogue; but this is not expressed in the terms they use to indicate the peculiar character of the Holy Scriptures. Where we employ the word "canonical," therefore, in the present enquiry, especially in connexion with the discussions of the Jewish schools, it must be taken with this qualification. The scientific use of this word in such investigations as ours is well established.

² To signify that a writing is what we should call "canonical," the Talmud says that it "defiles the hands." We remain of this opinion, notwithstanding the fact that J. S. Bloch (*Studien zur Gesch. d. Sammlung d. althebr. Lit.*, 1876, p. 152 f.) loftily assures us that it is "positively an error" to connect this designation "with the formation of the Canon or even with the canonical character of a book." His argument is acute and confident enough, but not convincing. Let the reader only go through § 6, n. 5 and 6, above, and try to substitute for this phrase anything else than "canonical." Upon this theory, moreover, it must be supposed to be accidental that the phrase is used, for example, of a book such as Ecclesiastes, of the controversy about which Jerome (§ 7 n. 4) is still aware. Bloch's assertions are intended to prove that the Kethubim were at an early date firmly established. In his zeal to accomplish this he treats the passage *Megilla* fol. 7*a*, quite unfairly, representing that R. Samuel merely affirms that Esther was inspired by

---

* [Prol. in Cant.; ed. Delarue III, p. 36.]

the Holy Ghost; whereas there is unquestionably a tradition of this Samuel that Esther does not "defile the hands." (See § 6 n. 6.)

In later Jewish writings it is also customary to say simply קבלת הספר בין הכתובים (the book is received among the Scriptures), but in the Talmud the expression uniformly used of Holy Scriptures is that they are מטמאים את הידים (*Yadaïm* iii. 5, iii. 6; *Megilla* fol. 7*a*; *Eduyoth* v. 3; *Shabbath* fol. 14*a* &c.) For the explanation of this peculiar and strange sounding expression see, for example, Weber, *System der altsynagogalen Paläst. Theologie*, Leipzig, 1880, p. 82, [subsequently also under the title, *Lehren des Talmud,*]). According to the rabbinic explanation, the place where the Holy Scriptures lay was declared unclean, in order that there-after no one should deposit Teruma there (as had formerly been done because they wished, in accordance with *Shabbath* fol. 14*a*, to lay holy things by the side of holy), and so attract mice which might get to gnawing the holy book and thus injure it. The holy book must in no case come into contact with other things since it was קדש. In order to guard against this, they attributed to the holy book טמאה; for in this way everything was kept away from it, since by contact with it every other object would also become טמאה, and would then have to be purified.

Graetz, *Kohelet*, p. 160 [cf. 166 f.] offers a different explanation, derived from *Yadaïm* iv. 6, which at the same time makes it clear why this term is never applied to the Law or Prophets, but only to Kethubim. The Sadducees said to Rabban Johanan ben Zakkai: "We complain of you Pharisees, because you say that Holy Scriptures defile the hands, but the writings of Homer (Graetz translates: books relating the day's events, journals) * do

---

* [On the word המירס (*v.l.* המירם, המירום) see Levy, *Nh.Wb.* I. 476, III 245; "Homer" is certainly an error.]

not." Johanan replied: "Is that all that you have against the Pharisees? Why, they also say that the bones of an ass are clean, while the bones of the high priest Johanan (John Hyrcanus) are unclean." They answered: "The uncleanness is in proportion to the estimation in which they are held, to prevent a man's making a spoon of his father's or mother's bones." He replied to them: "The same rule applies to the Holy Scriptures; their uncleanness is in proportion to their preciousness ([according to the parallel in the Tosephta; cf. *Nidda* 55*a*] to prevent their being used to make coverings for animals), whereas the writings of Homer, for which we have no affection, do not defile the hands." According to this interpretation of the singular rule, the intention was to preserve the Holy Scriptures from profanation. For the Law and the Prophets it was not necessary to make such a rule. Nevertheless the strange rule was certainly applied to other books than those of the third division; see *Kelim* xv. 6 (Bloch, *Studien*, p. 153), where an exception is made only for the copy (of the Tora) used by the high priest in the temple. Probably Graetz is so far right, that the rule was first made for the Kethubim.

Geiger's interpretation, also *(Nachgelassene Schriften,* 5 Bde., Berlin 1875—1878, IV. p. 14; cf. *Urschrift und Uebersetzungen der Bibel,* u. s. w., Breslau, 1857, p. 135), corroborates the opinion that this strange expression certainly refers to the holiness of the books. He rejects the explanation from *Shabbath* fol. 14*a* (quoted by Weber, p. 82) as "palpably absurd." According to him the Pharisees wished to make the regulations about clean and unclean less burdensome, and therefore decided, among other things, that the skins even of unclean animals, when dressed, did not make him who touched them unclean. In the solitary case of the leather on which sacred books were written they maintained the older, stricter rule, reconciling themselves to the inconsistency. The "temple-court copy" (ספר העזרה)

from which the high priest read on the great Day of Atonement, was excepted (*Kelim* xv. 6), because it was written upon leather ceremonially clean. The explanation given by Fürst (*Kanon*, p. 83): "They declare the hands to be unclean, unless previously washed," is altogether arbitrary and incorrect.

A writing which does not "defile the hands" must be "hid away." The Hebrew word for this is גנז. At first sight this seems to be exactly equivalent to ἀποκρύπτειν; and ספרים גנוזים would thus mean precisely the same as *libri apocryphi*. This is, however, incorrect. It must be remarked, in the first place, that the Jewish term comprehends much less than our expression, apocryphal books. Compare Fürst, *Kanon des A. T.* p. 127, n. 1; 148, n. 1; 150. What we (since Jerome)* especially call apocryphal books, i. e. writings which do not belong to the Canon at all, the Jews comprise under the name חיצונים [libri extranei]. Among the Hisonim are also the books of Maccabees (מגלות בית השמונאי), Sirach (סירא בן משלות), Wisdom (חכמת שלמה) and the Haggadas Daniel, Judith, and Tobit. These are at least never called ספרים גנוזים. The words *ganaz*

---

* Before Jerome *libri apocryphi* was understood partly of secret writings of heretics, partly of pseudepigrapha. The books which since Jerome have been denominated apocrypha, i.e. those which the manuscripts of the LXX usually include over and above what are found Hebrew Bible, were before him called βίβλια ἀναγινωσκόμενα, *libri ecclesiastici*, because they were read in church. (See Keil, *Einleitung in das A. T.*, 3 ed. § 226.) Jerome's translation of this Jewish term is only in so far right, that for him also the point of the question is, whether certain books which were already publicly read at religious services, should be regarded as Sacred Scripture. But the controversy in the case of the Church Father did not concern the same books as that in the Jewish Schools. Cf. also Buhl, *Kanon und Text*, p. 60; Engl. trans., p. 60 f.).

and *ganuz* are only used of some of our well-known canonical books, as to which, for one reason or another, the question was raised whether they ought not rather to be "hid away." Thus a Tora roll which has become dirty is also "hid away." (Buhl, *Kanon und Text* p. 7; Engl. transl. *p.* 7.) The discussions make altogether the impression, as Nöldeke (*Die alttest. Literatur*, Leipzig, 1868, p. 238) has justly remarked, that the disputed books were in use, but that objections had been raised against their use in the synagogue. Accordingly the question was not, shall the books be accepted? but rather, should they not be withdrawn.

In every synagogue the Tora only is kept in the sacred chest, called תיבה, ארון, or כתר תורה (crown of the law). In this, the rolls, properly wrapped in linen cloths and enclosed in a תיק ($\vartheta\eta\varkappa\eta$), are deposited. If a book was judged suitable for public reading (לקריאה), it obtained no place in the תיבה (at least not in later times; cf § 11 n. 2), but was kept in a little box on the reading desk (בימה, $\beta\eta\mu\alpha$) or elsewhere in the synagogue, and might be read there beside the Tora. A book which was not esteemed worthy of this honor was relegated, just as a Tora roll was which had become in some way defective, to the *Geniza*, the lumber-room of the synagogue. (Cf. *Sopherim* iii. 9; W. Robertson Smith, *Old Testament in the Jewish Church.* 2 ed. p. 71 n. 1. Wellhausen in Bleek's *Einleitung* [4] p. 551; Strack, *Prolegomena Critica in Vet. Test. Hebr.*, Lipsiae, 1873, p. 42).

We see, thus, that the apocrypha proper, which were wholly foreign to the use of the Synagogue (*Hisonim*), are not even included in the name *Sepharim genuzim*. They had never been thought of in authoritative Jewish schools for reading in the synagogue. But the Kethubim were manifestly, in the leading synagogues, deemed worthy a place beside the Tora. And it was this which some rabbis could not admit without question

But they could not persist in opposition to the general usage, and either silently yielded or sought to justify this usage.

One more remark. It may be objected to the representation we have given, that our evidence does not show that, beside the Law, anything was read in the Synagogue except certain parts of the Prophets (54 Haphtaras) and—on the five appointed festivals—the five Megilloth. It is true that officially nothing else is prescribed. But must not a freer practise have preceded the official prescription? And did the obligation to read the required passages leave no liberty to read more? Compare § 10, n. 9 and § 11, n. 7. The Jews of Nehardea were accustomed to read portions of the Kethubim at the Sabbath evening service; *Shabbath* 116*b*. When Tertullian (*de cultu femin* i. 3) says of the book of Enoch, "nec in armarium judaicum admittitur," this expression supposes the possibility that besides the Tora, the Haphtaras, and the five Megilloth, other sacred books also might be read in the synagogue. See as to the admission to the "armarium judaicum" § 11, n. 2.

The real touchstone of canonicity for Old Testament books was the Tora. The Jewish scholars are profuse in proclaiming its praises and its altogether unique signifiance [3]. It is properly canonical in the highest sense of the word. The rest of the books derive their value solely from it, and are of importance only as an explanation and further elucidation of the Tora [4]. To such a degree is this the case, that the whole Old Testament is cited by Jewish scholars as the Law [5]. While, thus, a book which was regarded as in conflict with the Tora, could not be tolerated, it did not follow that every book which agreed with the spirit of the Tora would be accepted. Other reasons beside this determined a favorable or unfavorable decision in the case of some books. If a work was attributed to some celebrated man of ancient times, it might be received. If the author was a well-known person of later times, it would be excluded. For this reason very probably the Proverbs of Jesus ben Sirach were not admitted to the canon [6]. Further, historical books must relate to the classical period in order to be considered candidates for admission. For this reason the First Book of Maccabees did not get a place in the Canon [7].

[3] The reader may get an idea of the extraordinary praises bestowed on the Tora and of the importance ascribed to it by the Jews, from Weber, *System der altsynagogalischen Palåst. Theologie* [*Lehren des Talmud*] p. 1—60. Out of the depths of the divine essence, before time was, the Wisdom of God appeared before Him, and this Wisdom is identical with the Tora. So chiefly in older and later Midrashim; but also in Jesus ben Sirach, c. 24. After the eulogy of Wisdom, existent from eternity, he proceeds thus in vs. 23 (32): "All these things are * the book of the covenant of God Most High; the Law, which Moses commanded for an heritage unto the congregations of Jacob". Preëxistence is thus attributed to it; it is called the daughter of God; yea, God himself occupies himself with the Tora (Weber,

* [Syr., *written in.*]

l. c. p. 14 f.). For man it is the source of all well being, and the highest good; the source of life, of light, of sanctification and of refreshing. It is חמדה מתוך חמדה, "the jewel of jewels" (*ib.* p. 20 f.). "Whoever asserts that the Tora is not from heaven (*i. e.* from God). (אין תורה מן השמים), hath no part in the world to come" (*Sanhedrin* x. 1). "Whoever saith, that Moses wrote so much as a single verse out of his own knowledge (מפי עצמו), he (is a liar and) a contemner of the word of God" (*Sanhedrin* fol. 99a.) The only controverted point was whether God had revealed the whole Tora to Moses at once, or by successive parts (מגלה מגלה).

4) As the praise accorded to the Tora is altogether unique, so for the Jew the Law possesses an altogether unique character. It is far from being the case that the other Holy Scriptures stand upon an equality with it. The money, for instance, which is received from the sale of a Tora roll may not be expended for the purchase of other Holy Scriptures. We read in *Megilla* iii, 1, that if the men of a town sell a Tora they may not buy with its price the other books of Scripture; when they sell other Scriptures they may not buy cloths in which to wrap the Tora; when they sell such cloths they may not buy for them a chest in which to place the Synagogue rolls; when they sell a chest, they may not buy a synagogue for it; and when they sell a synagogue they may not buy a street for it (an open space for prayer, Matt. 6, 5)." See W. Robertson Smith, *Old Test. in the Jewish Church*, 2 ed. p. 161.

The Jews have thus not the slightest intention of putting the Nebiim and Kethubim on an equality with it, although the same formulas of Scripture quotation are used for all three groups. The Tora is properly cannonical in the highest sense of the word. It alone has the place of honor in the synagogue, in the תיבה, which is always placed directly opposite the entrance to the house of prayer. About it the entire ritual on the Sabbath is centred, and tokens of honour are shown it in the reading which are not observed in reading from other books of the Old-Testament. The Tora is in reality the sole saving revelation of God's ways, destined not only for Israel, but in the future for the Gentiles also. For this reason it is said in *Mechilta* [Par. יתרו init., ed. Weiss. 64*b*.] "When the Tora was given to Israel, all the kings of the earth trembled in their palaces (see Weber p. 18 f.). Yahwe's communion with Israel depends solely on the Tora (ib.p. 46 f.); and Israel as the people of the Law is the people of God (ib. p. 50 f.). "The Tora is therefore also a perfectly sufficient revelation. "If Israel had done right there would have been no need of any further revelation besides the Tora through Nebiim and Kethubim" (*Koheleth rabba* [on Eccles. 1.13; ed. Sulzb. 63*d*. Wünsche p. 21.] 63*d*.) So also on Deut. 30, 12," "Say not that another Moses will arise and bring another Tora from the heavens; there remaineth no other Tora besides in the heavens" (*Debarim rabba*, sec. 8 [ed. Sulzb. fol. 223 c; Wünsche p. 96]). It should be obsersed in this connection that the word *Tora* las the broad sense of instruction, so that the teaching of the prophets is also called *Tora*.

The other scriptures are contrasted with this revelation κατ' ἐξοχήν, as tradition (קבלה or אשלמתא). We have already seen how in the Mishna the book of Joel is cited as *kabbala* (§ 6, n. 8), and in Zunz, *Die gottesdienstl. Vorträge der Juden*, p. 44 n. a. (2*d* ed., p. 46, n. 6) a number of such citations from Nebiim and Kethubim will be found. The second and third divisions of the Bible were thus called *kabbala*, as well as the words of the scribes. They are distinguished from the latter only by the fact that they were spoken by the Holy Ghost; but inasmuch as they are still, as compared to the law, nothing more than its fuller explanation, they belong properly to tradition. It was the work of the prophets to transmit the oral law (cf. § 9, n. 8) which had been handed down from Moses to Joshua, from the latter to the elders, and from them to the prophets (*Aboth* i. 1). The mediæval Jewish scholars therefore distinguish very justly, from the Jewish point of view, the three divisions of the Old Testament Canon as the holy of holies, the holy place, and the outer-court (see Buhl, *Kanon und Text*, p. 4; Engl. trans. p. 4). In entire accord with this is the treatment they receive in the synagogue. The prophets are read in conjunction with the Law, but only as a conclusion or appendix to the reading of the Tora. The expository remarks, also, are chiefly occupied with the parasha of the Tora, and either not at all, or only in very slight degree, with the haphtara of the Nebiim. See Weber, *op. cit.*, p. 80, who observes further, that, in so far as there is in the Talmud anything that can be called criticism of the Holy Scriptures, it always has to do with the second or third divisions, never with the first.

The question whether a book is canonical or not, from the Jewish point of view amounts to this: Does it agree with the Revelation, that is, with the Tora, or not?

5 If the Tora is the highest, and in reality the all-sufficient revelation, it follows that the authors of the rest of the Holy Scriptures can have added nothing new to the Tora. And this is in fact the Jewish opinion. "Is there anything written in the Kethubim, that is not intimated in the Tora?" (*Taanith* fol. 9a). "No prophet may introduce anything new, which is not grounded on the Tora." (*Bammidbar rabba*, c. 10, *Ruth rabba* on 2, 4; ed. Sulzb. fol. 32a top; Wünsche, p. 33). Even that which the prophets were to prophesy in future time was already revealed from Sinai (Weber, p. 79).

This is, then, the reason why the whole O. T. is more than once called "the Law." It is not merely because the Jews regard the Tora as the oldest, the fundamental part of the Holy Scripture, or even as the highest in rank; but because it is *the* Revelation, and all the rest is looked upon either as *kabbala* or as simply a part of the Tora. The whole O. T. thus presents itself to the Jews as a law. So e. g., as a proof of the resurrection, Ps. 84, 5 is cited מן התורה (*Sanhed.* fol. 91*b*; Weber, p. 79); and in the same way in the New Testament, the Old Testament is cited as "the Law" in places where Psalms and Prophets are referred to; John. 10, 34. 12, 34. 15, 25. 1 Cor. 14, 21. (cf. § 5, n. 1.)

⁶ Had it sufficed for the admission of a book to the ranks of the Holy Scriptures, that it was not in conflict with the Tora, the Proverbs of Jesus ben Sirach should have attained a place of honour, for the author is profuse in extolling the praises of the Law. But this was not the case; and Sirach got no further than the border line between canonical and uncanonical books. Some indeed believe that it come within the line, and that even three centuries after Christ Jewish scholars still quote it as canonical (see e.g. Cheyne, *Job and Solomon*, 1887, p. 282 f). Augustine also (*de doctrina christiana*, ii. 8) was of this opinion, though he retracted it later. But against this it is to be said that not all passages from the Talmud are equally convincing; and that the rabbis, quoting from memory, may have adduced passages from this book, believing that they were citing actual texts of Scripture. This confusion might occur the more easily, because Jesus ben Sirach wrote in biblical style. (See Strack, in *P. R. E*². VII. 430 ff.). But even if, with Cheyne, we regard this as "too bold a conjecture," it would only follow that a very few rabbis put Sirach on the same plane with the Holy Scriptures. It never attained, however, to any general recognition; and no one ever counted twenty five in place of twenty four books for the sake of including Sirach. That there were some, however, who were not at all satisfied with the practise and the decision of the schools, appears from Akiba's passionate protestation that a man who reads Ben Sira or other Ḥisonim has no part in the world to come (*Jerus.*

Sanhedrin x. 1, fol. 28 *a*; cf *Bab. Sanhedr.* fol. 100 *b.**) Prof. Buhl (*Kanon u. Text*, p. 6, 8; Engl. transl. 6, 8,) believes that in this passage heretical and Jewish-Christian books were originally meant; but he admits that there were stricter rabbis who declared even the reading of such books as Sirach to be forbidden.

Why was Sirach not received into the Canon, while other books of about the same age found a place in it? The only satisfactory answer is, not that the Canon was then already closed (Fürst, *Kanon*, p. 65, n. 7,), but that the author's name was known, and that the work of a living man could not be esteemed worthy of this exceptional honor. It must not be forgotten, moreover, that such a book, which in other respects did not accord with the views of the scribes (it contains nothing about the doctrine of angels, or of Satan, or of the resurrection), would not be universally relished. These doctrines are indeed not found in Ecclesiastes either; but it bore the name of the famous King Solomon, and under his name succeeded in gaining authority, although subsequently men were astonished and scandalized that it had done so.

And Daniel, although in its present form the book was not written until about 165 B. C., was not excluded, because its principal character was a well-known figure of the exile (Ezek. 14, 14. 20 and 28, 3).

7 Historical books were not admitted, unless they related to the classical period. After the exile this was over, and the collection of the spiritual treasures of Israel was begun. Whatever related to pre-exilic times, or dealt with the history of the exile and as its conclusion described the establishment of the Jewish community in Palestine, must have a place in the series of sacred books. Thus such late books as Chronicles, Ezra-

---

* [On the text of these passages see the ref. in Buhl, *l. c.*]

Nehemiah, and even Esther were included. But the contents of 1 Maccabees fell outside these limits.

Other reasons have been sought for the exclusion of 1 Maccabees. Some discover the cause in the fact that the Canon was already closed. But we have already learned how little ground there is for this opinion. Others think that 1 Macc., as well as Sirach, was not included because the Hebrew original had been lost. But we know that Jerome, in the fourth century of our era, had seen 1 Macc. in Hebrew; and various passages of the Talmud show acquaintance with the משלות בן סירא. See § 7, n. 3. Origen, also, knew the Hebrew title of 1 Macc., *Sarbeth Sar bane El*, Σαρβήθ Σαρβαναιέλ (Euseb., *Hist Eccl.*, vi, 25; see Dyserinck, *De Apocriefe Boeken des O. V.*, p. xv. f). If the explanation proposed be not accepted, the most probable view would be that the book was rejected by the scribes on account of its anti-pharisaic tendency. So Abr. Geiger, *Urschrift und Uebersetzungen der Bibel*, p. 201. Dyserinck also, *op. cit.* p. xix, gives the preference to this view, and mentions only in the second place the alternative opinion which we defend. The reason we have given is, however, decisive, even if we must admit that the scribes, with their Pharisean leanings, would not be much prepossessed with 1 Maccabees. But had the book been excluded solely on account of its tendency, they ought to have admitted 2 Maccabees, which has a strong Pharisean colouring, and is often so directly opposed to the views of 1 Maccabees as to give Geiger reason for thinking that it purposely wages a polemic against it. This is also the opinion of Dr. W. H. Kosters, in his article, "De polemiek van het tweede boek der Makkabaeën, *Theol. Tijdschrift*, 1878, p. 491—558; see however, Schürer, *Geschichte d. Jud. Volkes*, u. s. w. II. p. 740; *Hist. of the Jewish People*, 2d. Div. Vol. III. p. 212.

§ 9.

HISTORY OF THE COLLECTION OF THE OLD TESTAMENT BOOKS.

a. THE CANONIZATION OF THE LAW.

The history of the canonization of the Old Testament books commences with the canonization of the Tora by Ezra (444 B. C.). But its real beginning lies before the exile in the covenant concluded by King Josiah (621 B. C.) on the basis of the book of Deuteronomy. The Law of Deuteronomy was, therefore, for a little while before the Babylonian exile, during the exile, and for a considerable period after it, Israel's first "Holy Scripture."[1]

---

[1] Cf. § 3, n. 3. We cannot describe the history of the collection of the O. T. books without assuming results of historical criticism which we regard as established. But our enquiry does not depend upon these results, although it coincides with them remarkably. It should be remembered, moreover, that we have to do not so much with the making of the laws as with the sanction by which they were declared to be binding. In our opinion the conception and the promulgation of the laws are closely connected in time; but for our purpose it is comparatively indifferent whether a latent existence be ascribed to the laws of the Tora before their promulgation or not. See Wellhausen, *Einleitung* 4, p. 556, n. 1, for the proof that

Josiah did not introduce the whole Pentateuch, but Deuteronomy only. In regard to the most recent objections to this view, brought forward by M. Vernes (*Une nouvelle hypothèse sur la composition et l'origine du Deutéronome*, Paris, 1887), see my acticle in *Theol. Studiën*, 1887, p. 238 ff., and Kuenen, *Theol. Tijdschrift*, 1888, p. 35 ff.

The question is, whether we are right in recognizing in the narrative of the introduction of Deuteronomy in the eighteenth year of Josiah (2 Ki. 22. 23) the canonization of a portion of the Law. Objections may be urged against this view; we may, for instance, be pointed to the fact that Josiah's efforts had no such permanent results as those of Ezra had later; that the idea of Tora could not have been so firmly established, otherwise it would have been impossible that nearly a century after the exile so important a part should have been added to it as was done by Ezra. Above all, it may be argued that the conception of a Canon presupposes a church, and that Israel did not become a church until after the exile.

To begin with this last objection. It is perfectly true, that Canon and church belong together, and before the great catastrophe Judah, however insignificant, was still a nation. But we must remember that precisely the book of Deuteronomy aimed at the creation of a church, and worked to this end; in other words, it purposed to transform the national organization into one mainly religious. Deuteronomy is an attempt to realize Isaiah's ideal of the holy people (Is. 4, 3. 6, 13. 11, 1—9 &c.). Cheyne justly says (*Jeremiah: his life and times*, p. 73), "The author of Deuteronomy and his friends, with not inferior earnestness though with less rigor than Ezra, attempted the bold experiment (bold, for any but prophets and the disciples of prophets) of converting a nation into a church, and an earthly kingdom into a theocracy."

That the efforts of the Deuteronomist and his followers had

not the permanent results which afterwards crowned the work of Ezra, was due not so much to the fact that they undertook the work less vigourously, for Josiah went to work with unsparing thoroughness,—but to the fact that the times were not ripe for it. The nationality, although nearing its end, was still too strong, the life too full and rich, to bind itself absolutely to the letter. The testimony of Yahwé was still heard from the mouth of a Jeremiah, and hence could not be regarded as wholly concluded in "the book of the Law."

But how was it possible, then, it may be asked, that nearly two centuries later so important a part as the Priestly Law could be added to this Sacred Scripture? It is to be observed, as to this, 1. that Deuteronomy presupposes an (oral) priestly tora (Deut. 24, 8. 17, 18. 31, 9). That this tora should, after two centuries, be accepted as Scripture involves no improbability. 2. The first period of canonization must not be regarded as an age entirely devoid of spontaneous activity. The Priestly law also, as we shall show, was expanded after its introduction. The acceptance of Deuteronomy as authoritative Scripture, like the canonization of the Priestly law at a later time, was at once the close of a preceding development and the beginning of a new period. The Deuteronomic writers are conscious that Israel's national existence is approaching its end. The exile is the black background to which they are drawing ever nearer. This dark future is the punishment which is denounced both in Deuteronomy and in the Deuteronomic books of Samuel and Kings.

In this consciousness they set about collecting the older literature. Thus the books of Judges, Samuel, and Kings (the redaction of which was completed after the Exile) have been transmitted to us in Deuteronomic garb. But, as usual in Oriental historiography, their collecting was at the same time reworking. The same process was repeated after the year 444.

Then the Deuteronomic historical books were preserved as Sacred Scriptures, and under the impulse of the newer (priestly) conception, the history was worked over in a priestly sense. This was the course of the post-exilic historiography, which ended in the composition of the books of Chronicles, Ezra, Nehemiah.

Finally, the question may be raised, whether, if we commence with Deuteronomy, the history of canonization must not begin still earlier, with the Book of the Covenant (Ex. 20, 23—23, 33). We know nothing certainly about any promulgation of the Book of the Covenant. It must have had a private character; for Deuteronomy, which often closely follows its prescriptions, nowhere mentions it.* It was also evidently compiled for the use of those who were engaged in the administration of justice, and is not a book for the people, like Deuteronomy. But Deuteronomy is "Sacred Scripture." It is highly probable that Jeremiah was one of those who preached this book (Jer. 11; cf. Cheyne, *Jeremiah*, p. 55 f.); and the traces of its influence are plainly demonstrable even down to Ezra, who resolves to send away the foreign wives on the ground of the law in Deuteronomy (Ezra 10, 3).

The Jews who returned from the exile under Zerubbabel the Prince and Joshua the High Priest really no longer formed a nation, but a religious community. This community had already existed since the year 536 B. C. (edict of Cyrus), when in

---

* [It almost certainly originated in Ephraim, and if promulgated could have had no authority in the southern kingdom, though preserved together with other Ephraimite literature after the destruction of Samaria. — B. W. B.]

458 Ezra, the priest and scribe "proficient in the Law of Moses" (Ezra 7, 6), came up from Babylon with a great company of zealous co-religionists, to support and reënforce the community in Jerusalem. He came with the Law of his God in his hand (Ezra 7, 14. 25); but did not introduce this Law until 444, when Nehemiah, a man of kindred spirit, had become the Persian governor (445—433). From 536 to 444, nearly a hundred years, Deuteronomy, the Law book which the Jews had taken with them into the exile, continued to be their Sacred Scripture. Even before the return from the Exile, however, following in the steps and in the spirit of Ezekiel, schools of jurisprudence had been formed in Babylon, which, in firm faith in the glorious restoration of the nation, compiled and worked over the priestly traditions[2]. Such priestly laws, whether oral or written, certainly enjoyed a high esteem in the community of Joshua and Zerubbabel. But they did not acquire canonical authority until Ezra in 444, on the first day of the seventh month, publicly read, in the market-place before the Water-gate, a complete system of priestly laws, and the people solemnly pledged themselves to live according to these laws (Neh. 8—10)[3]. Combined with the previously existing scripture (Deuteronomy), the entire Tora has been from

Ezra's time down, Israel's Holy Scripture. Now that the priestly laws also were no longer handed down orally but were fixed in writing, Israel became for all the future a "people of the book"[4]. It cannot be proved that any other books attained to canonical authority at the same time with the Law. The historical account in Neh. 8—10 speaks of the Tora only. In confirmation of this is the further fact that the Samaritans have accepted as Holy Scripture nothing but the Law (and the book of Joshua); while, finally, the absolute unique honour in which the five books of Moses are held by the Jews corroborates this view[5].

[2] The representation of the course of events in this period as given in the text, has been recently defended against the objections which have at various times been made to it, by Kuenen, in his article, "De Chronologie van het Perzische Tijdvak der Joodsche Gesch, in *Versl. en Meded. d. Koninkl. Akad.*, Afd. Letterk., 3e Reeks, Deel vii., 1890, p. 273—322. Nehemiah came as successor to Sheshbazzar (Ezra 1, 11), who is not to be identified with Zerubabel. The regulation of internal affairs in Judaea was probably entrusted to a man of the ruling nation. (Kuenen, p. 282 f.).

For our purpose it is again practically indifferent, what in the priestly laws is old, and what of recent date. See my article in *Theol. Studiën*, 1887, p. 341—355. It is enough to know that the priestly laws were zealously studied in the exile, and that such a man as Ezekiel concludes his book with the draught of a law for the nation on its return (ch. 40—48).

a. THE CANONIZATION OF THE LAW.

From the days of Ezekiel, who was carried into captivity in 597, the leaders of the Jews in Babylon continued zealously occupied with the study of the law, even after 536. During this long period there was manifestly no lack of priests like Ezekiel and Ezra, who might at the same time be called scribes, "proficient in the Law of Moses." Such a man was, for instance, the redactor of the collection preserved to us in Lev. 17—26, often called the "Law of Holiness." Others worked over other ordinances; and Ezra could be called a man well versed in such legal study, which, we must not forget, had already been cultivated in Babylon for more than a century. Arrived in Jerusalem, he most probably, in the years between his own coming (458) and that of Nehemiah (445), continued to busy himself with the study of the Tora, in order to prepare for the introduction of the Law.

3 The detailed account of the introduction of the Law is to be read in Neh. 8—10; that is, in a narrative written by the Chronicler, who lived about 250 B.C. Nevertheless this passage is of great historical value. It is distinguished by vividness of description, and was not written by the Chronicler but incorporated by him from an older source, as is evident from its discrepant presupposition that the law to the observance of which the people pledged themselves under Ezra did not comprise all the ordinances which are now found in it. (Cf. n. 4; and see a defense of the historical importance and credibility of this section against Zunz, *Die gottesd. Vorträge der Juden*, p. 24—26, and others, by Kuenen *H. C. O²*., I. p. 509 f).

On the first day of the 7th month (the year is not named, but the event took place manifestly but a short time after Nehemiah's coming), a great popular assembly was held in the open court before the Water-gate, where Ezra was to read publicly the book of the Law of Moses. Early in the morning Ezra began the reading from a wooden pulpit, while seven priests were ranged on his right hand and his left. The effect was general and profound sadness, because they now learned how far they had been from fulfilling the will of God. On the following day the reading was continued in the presence of the "heads of the fathers" (heads of the families), and they discussed the feast which they were required to keep just at this time, on the 15th of the 7th month, — the feast of Tabernacles. This feast was celebrated during eight days, as is ordained in Lev. 23, 39 (contrary to Deut. 16, 13—15, which fixed its duration at seven days), and every day they read out of the "book of the Law of God" (Neh. 8, 18). The 24th was a great fast day. After the fast day, they devoted yet another fourth part of the day to reading from the law, and a fourth part to acts of penitence (Neh. 9, 3). Thus they prepared themselves for the great day on which all the officers and elders of the people, in the name of the whole people, pledged themselves in writing to live in accordance with Ezra's law book (Neh. 10, 29).

The written priestly laws, intended chiefly for the priests, were now adopted as a book for the people also. In Neh. 10, 30—39, accordingly, those prescriptions with which the people have to do are put in the foreground, especially the raising of revenues for the multitude of priests.

4 Ezra probably had before him on his wooden pulpit only the priestly elements of the Pentateuch (or Hexateuch). This was the judgment of Reuss (*l'Histoire Sainte et la Loi*, I. p. 256, ff.; *Geschichte der Heiligen Schriften A Ts.*, 1881, § 377, p. 460 f.; 2e Ausg. 1890, p. 485 f.); and now of Kuenen also, (*H. C. O².*, I. p 217 n. 11, p. 295 n. 25 = *Hexateuch*, p. 223, n. 11, p. 304 n. 25), contrary to his earlier opinion (*Religion of Israel*, II. p. 229 ff.). The work of editing the Hexateuch, i. e. of combining the new law with the existing Sacred Scripture, the Deuteronomy, to which the pre-Deuteronomic or prophetic elements had certainly been already added, took place some-

what later. But the manner in which the redaction was done proves that the Deuteronomic and pre-Deuteronomic portions already enjoyed undisputed authority, and that the union of the younger with the older parts was effected for the purpose of more firmly establishing the recently acquired authority of the priestly sections. See Kuenen, *H. C. O.*² I. p. 309 f. = *Hexateuch*, p. 319 ff. Ezra thus, properly speaking, only assured canonical authority to the Priestly Law, as had been done for Deuteronomy in the reign of Josiah. Moreover the Priestly Law was not then as extensive as now. The requirement of the daily evening sacrifice (Exod. 29, 38—42, Num. 28, 1—9); of the poll-tax to the amount of a half shekel (Exod. 30, 11—16); and of the tithe of cattle (Lev. 27, 32—33), were added to it later. In Nehemiah's days, after the introduction of the Priestly Law, these prescriptions had not yet been made, as appears from Neh. 10, 34. 10, 33 and 10, 38—40 (12, 44—47, 13, 5. 12). See Kuenen *Rel. of Isr.* III. p. 6 f. 49 ff., and *H. C. O.*², I. 300 f. n. 30 = *Hexateuch*, p. 309 ff., n. 30. Still, we may safely say that from Ezra's time on the Tora as a whole enjoyed canonical authority; for the pre priestly parts were already esteemed sacred. Only it must not be overlooked that the period immediately following the canonization of the Law was not in such bondage to the letter as later times. The generation which had witnessed its canonization, did not yet look upon the Law as a dead relic, but rather as the reduction to writing of the will of God, as it had been learned in the course of the centuries from the mouth of His interpreters. Compare Ezra 9, 11 f., where a commandment which we find in Lev. 18, 25. 27 and Deut. 7, 3 is attributed to "God's servants, the prophets." The free handling of the text, also, in this period,—not only of Nebiim and Kethubim but of the Tora also,—proves that the first generation following the canonization were not such slaves of the letter as the later generations of scribes. See on the text of Exod. 35.

40, Popper, *Der bibl. Bericht über die Stiftshütte*, Leipzig, 1862; and Kuenen, *H. C. O.*², I. p. 77 f. = *Hexateuch*, p. 76 ff.

Thus the Jewish people becomes with Ezra more and more a "people of the book" (*ahlu 'lkitāb*,) as Mohammed afterward named the peoples which possessed a Sacred Scripture and therefore might he tolerated (*Koran*, iii. 57, &c.)

⁵ That we cannot establish more about Ezra's part in the canonization of the Old Testament scriptures than that he invested the first five books with normative authority, must be admitted. See the proof of this in Kuenen, *H. K. O*¹, III. p. 429 f. Kuenen's arguments are: 1. The historical evidence justifies no other conclusion. We certainly cannot let later accounts and conjectures, such as appear in 4 (2) Esdras, counterbalance a historical document such as we possess in Neh. 8 — 10. 2. The Samaritans have as Sacred Scripture nothing but the Tora. At what time they adopted this is uncertain. Josephus (*Antt. Jud.* xi. 7, 2; xi. 8, 2—4; xiii. 9, 1) puts the founding of the temple on Gerizim in the time of Alexander the Great, 333 B. C. But the account has so great similarity to Neh. 13, 28 that it is a generally accepted opinion that the temple was founded, and therefore probably the Law introduced, about 80 years earlier (see Oort, *Laatste Eeuwen*, I. p. 13.) Why did the Samaritans accept no other books, for example, that of the Ephraimite prophet, Hosea — of Joshua we shall speak directly —. The answer must be: Because at the end of the 5th century no other authoritative sacred writings existed. As regards Joshua, the Samaritans possessed, at least in later times, a book of Joshua, which Juynboll edited with translation and commentary, from a manuscript furnished to Scaliger by Egyptian Samaritans in 1584. (*Chronicon Samaritanum Arabice conscriptum, cui titulus et liber Josuae*, Lugd. Batav., 1848.) This book has but very slight resemblance to our canonical book of Joshua. It is really the beginning of a chronicle relating the history down to the time of the Roman

emperors. Besides, the close connection of Joshua with the Pentateuch, taken together with the fact that Joshua is peculiarly the tribal hero of Ephraim, makes this exception quite explicable. 3. In connection with the other phenomena, the peculiar reverence of the Jews for the Tora becomes a strong proof of the earlier canonicity of these first five books of the Bible. It is probable, indeed, that it was only after the lapse of considerable time that other books were added to this sacred canon. For had the Prophets been canonized at the same time as the Law, the one-sided legalism of Ezra could not have developed itself so strongly.

The work of Ezra (Nehemiah), although not accomplished without strong opposition [5], had permanent results, because it answered the demands of the age [7]. But the stream of legal rules, which from the nature of the case went on expanding, could not be shut off by any official decree. When the time came that the Law was regarded as definitively fixed, this stream sought outlet by another channel, and there arose the ordinances of the "oral law" [8].

[6] That not all members of the Jewish community were pleased with the stringent measures for separation from the heathen, and so disapproved the way in which Ezra and Nehemiah sought to realize the idea of "the holy people of Yahwe", may be plainly seen in the story of the expulsion of the grandson of Eliashib, who had married a daughter of the Samaritan

Sanballat. This man, whose name according to Josephus was Manasseh, is thought to have founded the temple on Gerizim; see above, n. 5. Josephus' account is obviously based upon Neh. 13, 28 (cf. Oort, *Laatste Eeuwen* I. p. 13). A nobler and more spiritual opposition may, however, also have been made. We perhaps possess documentary evidence of it in the books of Ruth and Jonah, which in the opinion of some were written in this period.

7 The fact that Ezra, in spite of the opposition still gained his end, was due not only to his own strong personality and to the fact that he could rely upon the support of his powerful ally Nehemiah, but chiefly to the fact that he gave expression to the spirit of the age. The Jewish nation had become a church, and as such had urgent need of a written word of God. The oral tora was beginning to fail. The witness of prophecy became feebler and more infrequent—a point to which we shall recur in a subsequent paragraph. The feeling was general, that an important epoch was closed; hence men set about the work of collection and redaction, in order thus to make the spiritual treasures of the past serve the needs of the present and the future. This consciousness, which we have already observed in the exile, was still stronger in the post-exilic community. Ezra succeeded because he was the exponent of the needs of his age.

8 We have already seen that the canonization of the Law by Ezra did not at once arrest the stream of legal regulations (n. 4). But it lay in the nature of the case, that gradually the existing Scripture should come to be regarded as so fixed that no new regulations could be received into it. If necessity gave rise to such rules, they must find a place elsewhere. Thus e. g. the most recent definition of the age at which the Levites entered upon their service found a place in the books of Chronicles. The case is this: In Num. 4, 35, thirty years is the age required. In Num. 8, 23—26 this requirement is already reduced

a. THE CANONIZATION OF THE LAW.

to twenty five years, probably because the need had increased.*
But when later it was desired to reduce it to twenty years, this
rule could no longer be introduced into the Tora as a novel;
and therefore the modified practise was incorporated in the work
of the Chronicler (about 250 B. C.), in 1 Chron. 23, 24—27,
where it is legitimated as an ordinance enacted by David.

But this was not the case with all the new prescriptions. It
belongs to the nature of every system of law that it must con-
tinually expand. New cases are always coming up, for which
provision must be made; new questions are always arising which
must be answered. In point of fact, Ezra's Law, although it
provided for many cases, left the scrupulous Jew here and there
in a quandary. Thus they ran the risk at every moment of
involuntarily transgressing the Law. It must be protected against
this danger. The Jewish scholars term this, "hedging about,"
and speak of a סְיָג about the Law (*Aboth* i. 1). Such new
and more minute rules were given in the synagogue, and are
called, in distinction from the written Tora, the oral Law, תּוֹרָה
שֶׁבְּעַל פֶּה. This oral law is, thus, a totally different thing
from the oral law in Israel's national life before the exile, which,
as we explained in note 7, began to disappear in the post-
exilic community. The pre-exilic oral law is the foundation
of Ezra's written Law; whereas the distinctive character of the
later oral law is that it is chiefly based upon the written
Law, and serves principally for its protection. It is called
Halacha, הֲלָכָה. This name is generally interpreted as "that
which is current," employed thus of the consuetudinary law.

---

* [Cf. Ezra 8, 15 ff. The degradation of the Levites in the legislation of
Ezekiel 44, 5—28 and the post exilic systems, as compared with their
position under the Deuteronomic, and still more the pre-Deuteronomic,
offered but small inducement to those unable to prove Aaronic descent to
leave Babylon for Jerusalem. B. W. B.]

So Schürer, *Geschichte des Jüdischen Volkes*, II. p. 270, *Hist. of the Jewish People*, 2d. Div., I. p. 332. A more correct interpretation is given by Strack, art. "Thalmud," *P. R. E²*., XVIII. p. 299, where he says: הלכה is properly the act of going, walking; tropically, 1, a walk (life) in accordance with the Law (so ὁδός Acts 9, 2. 19, 9. 23. 24, 22 = the Christian religion); 2, the Law in accordance with which the walk of life must be guided.

This oral law, although it contained new regulations and modified existing laws, meant to be nothing else than an expansion of the written Law and a protection against its infraction. It was not to be regarded as containing any thing new; nay, it was even represented as having come down from Moses by the side of the written Law. So *Aboth* i. 1; cf. *Pea* ii. 6; *Eduyoth* viii. 7; *Yadaïm* iv. 3. It is supposed to have been transmitted from Moses to Joshua, from the latter to the elders, from them to the prophets, and from these again to the men of the Great Synagogue. But this παράδοσις τῶν πρεσβυτέρων (Matt. 15, 2. Mark 7, 3) arose only after Ezra, for the purpose of making a "hedge" about the law; and was the channel in which the perennial stream of legal regulations had to flow.

§ 10.

HISTORY OF THE COLLECTION OF THE OLD TESTAMENT BOOKS, CONTINUED.

b. THE CANONIZATION OF THE PROPHETS.

Although we have not at our command, for the history of the canonization of the second division

b. THE CANONIZATION OF THE PROPHETS.

of the Old Testament books, any such historical testimony as we have for those of the Law, it is still possible for us, from various facts and statements, to form a conception of the course of events which agrees with these accounts and is supported by facts. We shall not seek in vain for an answer to the questions which here present themselves. 1. We shall enquire when this work began, and when it may be regarded as having reached completion. 2. What were the motives which led to this collection? 3. Who accomplished this work? 4. We shall endeavour to ascertain what can be learned of their method of work.

[1] That we have no historical testimonies concerning the origin of the collection of the Nebiim which are at all to be compared in value with the account in Neh. 8—10, is sufficiently apparent from the preceding paragraphs. The later Jewish conjectures in the Talmud can, because of this character, not be taken into consideration. Fürst did a useful work in collecting so much material in his *Kanon*, but it must be employed with more discrimination.

For the basis of the collection of the Nebiim (and other books) we must look to the work which according to 2 Macc. 2, 13 Nehemiah did. He collected, though with no intention of ascribing to them canonical authority, writings about the kings and the prophets; also Davidic psalms, and royal letters in regard to gifts to the temple. It is plain that this collection, both on account of its important contents, and on account of the standing of its author, must have been held in high esteem. It became the basis both of the second and of the third part of the Canon[2]. At what time the division of the Prophets was closed, we are not informed. But on account of Dan. 9, 2, whose author, living about 165 B. C., seems to know הַסְּפָרִים as a collection with definite limits, and because the book of Daniel itself was unable to obtain a place in the second section, we fix as a terminus ad quem about 200 B. C.[3] With this agrees the fact, that in the Prologue to the book of Sirach "the Prophets" or "the Prophetic Writings" appear as a division by the side of the Law[4]. The canonization of the prophetico-historical and other prophetic writings of the second section must, accordingly, be placed after Nehemiah and before the year 165 B. C.; probably about 200 B. C.

[2] See § 4, n. 6. It will be remembered that Nehemiah proposed to found a library, probably in the temple. It was therefore not in the least his intention to add a second Canon to that recently introduced; but he wished to preserve from destruction important documents, and also to have letters (probably from Persian kings) about gifts to the temple always within reach,

b. THE CANONIZATION OF THE PROPHETS.

in order that the Jews might be able to appeal to them upon occasion. We do not venture to name the books which found a place in this library. But that the prophetic books, Judges, Samuel, and Kings had a preëminent place in it, can scarcely be doubted. These, together with Joshua, constituted the Nebiim Rishonim (אשלמתא קדמייתא, Fürst, *Kanon*, p. 14, n. 7), as they were rightly called in later times, and were thus the foundation of the second division. What other writings were contained in it, and whether Nehemiah included even books such as Isaiah, Jeremiah, or Ezekiel, cannot be decided. Τὰ περὶ τῶν βασιλέων καὶ προφητῶν may very well apply solely to the prophetico-historical books. These were the books too, which were read by the post-exilic community with heightened interest. Their miserable condition, which answered so ill to the great expectations aroused in the exile, led them to read with avidity the stories of the glorious days of old, when a David or Solomon sat upon the throne, when prophets such as Elijah and Elisha exercised so great power and influence. For of this they were convinced, that all their suffering had come upon the people because of their sin. But if Israel now would only walk according to the commandments of Yahwe, the good old times would return, and much more glorious. "The sure mercies of David" (Is. 55, 3) were for the Israel of the future. In the mention of τὰ τοῦ Δαυίδ we see the foundation of the Kethubim; but on this point see the following paragraph.

3 See § 3, n. 6. By itself, Dan. 9, 2 does not prove much; but in connection with other phenomena we are justified in concluding that the writer of this apocalypse possessed a collecstion of prophetic writings with which he assumed that his readers also were acquainted. Of more weight is the circumstance that Daniel is not included among the Nebiim. The only reasonable explanation of this singular fact seems to be that,

when this book appeared, it was the universal opinion that the collection of the Prophets was irrevocably closed. The close of this division of the canon may, accordingly, have been reached about 200 B. C., if not somewhat earlier. We must not imagine that there was any official decision on the subject. Not a single statement or historical fact points to such a thing. We must also bear in mind that, although the collection of the Prophets was universally regarded as irrevocably closed, their canonical authority was not at once finally established.

[4] See § 4, n. 2. After the year 132 B. C., accordingly, the grandson of Jesus ben Sirach was acquainted, beside the Law, with οἱ προφῆται (αἱ προφητεῖαι) as a definite assemblage of books, while he is not acquainted with the third collection as such, though he knows a group of writings under a very indefinite name. Prof. Buhl (*Kanon und Text*, p. 12, Engl. trans., p. 12) mistakenly controverts my opinion by an appeal to Jesus ben Sirach himself, who wrote about 170 B. C. and who, as he thinks, recognized the Prophets as canonical; compare § 4, n. 1, where I think I have shown that Jesus ben Sirach did not recognize the Prophets as canonical. Doubtless, the tendency of opinion among many of his contemporaries, who were more inclined to Pharisaism than he, was in this direction; but he manifestly does not share this somewhat generally accepted view. The word "canonization" must therefore be taken in this connection also with some qualification; namely, not as an official decision by the competent authority, but as signifying that these books were regarded by the community and many of its leaders as sacred. For this, as is self-evident, no definite date can be given.

2. The motives which led to the canonization of other books beside the Tora are not altogether

the same as those which were operative in the canonization of the Law. Even before the exile there existed writings of the prophets which were eagerly read by the devout, and which, although they could not take the place of the living word, constituted an important complement to the spoken word [5]. In and after the exile they were much read, as appears, for instance from the writings of Deutero-Isaiah, Ezekiel and Zechariah [6]. That they were not at once formally declared sacred was doubtless due in part to the fact that they were not in so great need of this confirmation of their authority, but chiefly to the fact that they had not the same immediate importance for the establishment of Ezra's theocracy as the Priestly Law [7]. If our inference from 2 Macc. 2, 13 is correct, the canonization of the Nebiim had its origin in the felt necessity of collecting the important memorials of antiquity. It was felt that a momentous period was terminated, that a conflict which had lasted for centuries was ended; and when men became aware that the voice of prophecy had ceased to be uttered, they collected what were later called the Nebiim Acharonim also, and added them to Nehemiah's collection [8]. At about the same time we must probably also date the origin of the custom of reading from the Nebiim in the synagogue.

This custom was not a result of the work of Ezra, but was born of the insistence of the devout people, who were supported in this by their spiritual leaders in the searching of the Scriptures [9].

5 Before the exile the living word of the prophets had been the chief thing; but by the side of it prophetic writings also appear. As early as the 8th century B. C. a prophetic literature arose, — Amos, Hosea, Isaiah, Micah. In order to preserve the influence of their words the prophets themselves reduced their utterances to writing. Isaiah certainly himself put a part of his prophecies in writing and united them in a collection; although in the oracles preserved to us from him the hand of more than one later redactor is plainly recognizable (cf. n. 14 of this paragraph). And when, for the time being, he was unable to exert any influence by the spoken word, he expected to do so by the written word, at least among those who would listen to him: "Bind up the testimony, seal the (prophetic) tora among my disciples." (Is. 8, 16.)

6 Especially in and after the exile the prophets were much read. "When the national existence with which the ancient religion of Israel was so closely intertwined was hopelessly shattered, when the voice of the prophets was stilled, and the public services of the sanctuary no longer called the devout together, the whole continuance of the spiritual faith rested upon the remembrance that the prophets of the Lord had foreseen the catastrophe, and had shown how to reconcile it with undiminished trust in Jehovah, the God of Israel. The written word acquired a fresh significance for the religious life, and the books of the prophets, with those records of the ancient history which were either already framed in the mould of prophetic thought, or were cast in that mould by editors of the time of the Exile, became the main support of the faithful, who felt as they had

never felt before, that the words of Jehovah were pure words, silver sevenfold tried, a sure treasure in every time of need." (W. Robertson Smith, *O. T. in the Jewish Church*, 2 ed., p. 174).

The traces of acquaintance with prophetic writings are numerous both in the post-exilic Zechariah (see § 3, n. 8) and in the exilic prophets Ezekiel and Deutero-Isaiah. Ezekiel appeals formally to earlier prophets; perhaps sometimes to writings which for us are lost. He appears to be particularly dependent upon Jeremiah; cf. Ez. 2, 8 ff, with Jer. 1, 9; Ez. 13 with Jer. 23, 9—40; Ez. 18, 2 with Jer. 31, 29 ff, &c.; compare § 3, n. 5, and see further, Smend, *Der Prophet Ezechiel erklärt*, 1880, p. xxiv ff. Deutero-Isaiah also appeals to prophecies "from that time on", "from of old", "from eternity" (e. g. 46, 8—13), and it is very probable that in these appeals he is frequently thinking of such predictions as those of Jeremiah 25 and 29.

7 "These books had no need to be brought from Babylon with the approval of a royal rescript, or laid before the nation by the authority of a Tirshatha. The only form of public recognition which was wanting, and which followed in due course, was the practice of reading from the Prophets in the public worship of the synagogue. It required no more formal process than the natural use made of this ancient literature, to bring it little by little into the shape of a fixed collection." (W. Robertson Smith, *O. T. in the Jewish Church*, 2 ed. p. 175.

To this was added the fact—and this was the main thing—that for his purpose Ezra could not think of ascribing canonical authority to the prophets. Ezra wished to found a theocracy; it was an attempt to realize the prophetic idea of a holy people, consecrated to Yahwe. To this end, the demands of the prophets were stereotyped and adapted to every day circumstances in the Law. The Law of Deuteronomy was not sufficient, and so the system of the Priestly Law had grown up in accordance with the needs of the time. The people who pledged themselves to live according to its prescriptions were convinced that in this way they were also fulfilling the intentions of the prophets. Of another Canon besides the Law there can therefore be no question. The Law included the ideas and intentions of the prophets (Ezra 9, 11.)

⁸ There were thus properly two causes for the collecting of the Nebiim: 1. the desire to bring together the precious treasures of antiquity; and 2. the religious life of the devout in Israel, which was nurtured perhaps quite as much by the reading of the prophets as by the study of the Tora. We shall discuss this second cause in the note following (n. 9). Here we deal only with the former. There was a feeling in the post-exilic community that the period of revelation was closed (see § 9, n. 7). Malachi expects no such succession of prophets as is promised in Deut. 18, 18, but looks for salvation only through the return of the prophet Elijah (Mal. 4, 5. 6). In later days the appearance of a prophet is esteemed something so impossible that he who ventures to don the prophet's mantle, will at once be set down as an impostor (Zech. 13, 3., in our opinion a post-exilic prophecy). Compare also 1 Macc. 9, 27. 4, 46. See W. Robertson Smith, *O. T. in the Jewish Church*, 2 ed. p. 158 ff. The creative period was past, and the fact was keenly felt. Hence it came to pass that when any one had anything really new to say, he either did it under the name of some famous man of ancient times (pseudepigraphic writings, in which this period was so prolific), or in the form of paraphrase and fuller elucidation of existing texts. With the Halacha we have already become acquainted. Beside it appear the Midrash and the Haggada. In ancient times דרשׁ meant to enquire after the will of God at the mouth of a prophet or seer; see e. g. 2 Kings 1, 3. Later this will of God was sought in the written word, and this enquiry, together with its interpretation, was called Midrash. הַגָּדָה is the name for all appli-

cations of scripture which do not aim at establishment of legal rules. (Strack, art. "Thalmud," *P. R. E*². XVIII, p. 300.) * Jesus ben Sirach and the authors of Judith and Tobit are equally far from thinking that they are giving utterance to new religious ideas.

When the consciousness had thus become general that no more prophets would appear, the prophetic writings were collected and added to the collection of the Nebiim which had been in existence since the days of Nehemiah. It is quite possible that the memory of the interval between the canonization of the historical books and of the prophetic writings proper is perpetuated by the order of the two groups of books and by the appellation based upon it, *Nebiim Rishonim* and *Aharonim*. Von Orelli rightly observes, (*Theol. Literaturblatt*, May 13, 1892, p. 222), that, to judge from the citations of older prophets in younger authors, the writings of an Amos, an Isaiah, &c. were regarded "in a certain sense, as holy scriptures, as the word of God." Of course, as the spoken words of the prophets were the word of God, they were equally so when committed to writing. But that a second Bible, so to speak, was adopted beside the Tora must be explained in part by the fact that the voice of prophecy had became silent, and in part by the fact that the devout among the people and the profounder of the scribes were aware that not all the truth revealed by the prophets had been incorporated in the Law (cf. § 12, n. 3.)

9 Fürst (*Kanon*, p. 52) is partly right in opposing the opinion

---

* In the *Jewish Quarterly Review*, Vol. IV, 1892, p. 406—429, W. Bacher shows that in the oldest commentaries, *Mechilta* (on Exodus) and *Sifre* (on Numbers and Deuteronomy), הִגִּיד occurs in the sense of לִמֵּד. In the school of Ishmael this usage was common; in that of Akiba it was given up. According to Bacher, *Haggada* or *Aggada* (not Agada) means any teaching not halachic.

of later rabbis that the custom of reading haphtara lessons was first instituted in the time of Trajan or Hadrian as a substitute for the reading of the Law, which had been forbidden to the Jews. We say partly right, because he identifies the haphtara system with the "introduction of public lessons from the prophets." The latter was no doubt much earlier than the time of Trajan or Hadrian; but the establishment of the system of parallels from the prophets to the parashas of the Tora did not take place until after Christ. We know from the New Testament that in the days of Jesus and the apostles the Prophets were already regularly read in the synagogues, although not yet according to a fixed scheme of haphtaras, (cf. § 1, n. 7). On the other hand, the theory of Elias Levita (see Graetz, *Kohélet*, p. 157), that this custom originated in the Syrian period before the rise of the Maccabees, as a substitute for the reading of the Tora, the copies of which had been torn up and burned, is untenable But when did it begin? And from what side did it proceed? The reading of the lessons from the Prophets certainly did not begin immediately after Ezra, as Graetz (*Gesch. d. Juden*, II. 2, p. 191) asserts but does not prove. It is doubtless natural to think of the period of Syrian oppression. Then, no doubt, men encouraged themselves in the house of prayer with the word of prophecy. But why may they not have done so at a still earlier time? The godly in Israel, as appears from their utterances in the book of Psalms, lived in the word of prophecy; and why should they not have read it in the synagogue, though not at first by selected and appointed pericopes? The priests had less interest in this; for them it was enough that Ezra's theocracy had become a hierarchy. And they willingly resigned even instruction in the Tora to those of their colleagues who could be called by way of eminence 'scripturists' (scribes). But the godly people desired more. And when by degrees there comes to be a division into priests and scribes (of which we shall speak presently), it is plain that the latter are of one mind with the godly among the people. True, a veil lay upon their faces as they read the prophets; for from the point of view of the legalism which had prevailed since Ezra's time they could see nothing else in the prophets than interpreters of the Tora. But still they lent a willing ear to the insistence of the godly people, though they knew how to direct this movement into the path of legalism, to the great injury of spiritual life.

3. Although we are not expressly so informed, we have good grounds for holding that the canonization of other collections of books beside the Tora was the works of scribes of Jerusalem. We may infer this from what we know about the religious, political and social conditions of the period between Nehemiah and the Maccabees [10]. Furthermore, the fruits of their labors themselves give evidence to the same effect; as do also the well attested accounts of controversies over sacred character of certain books [11]. What the Jewish tradition relates (*Baba bathra* fol. 15a) about the labours of Ezra and the Men of the Great Synagogue rests upon an unhistorical conception which the later scribes entertained in regard to antiquity, and is very probably based upon the account of the popular assembly in Neh. 8—10 [12].

[10] In consulting the Jewish sources as to political conditions in earlier days we must be on our guard. The Talmudic ac-

counts all date from the time after the destruction of Jerusalem. At that time Israel's national existence came to an end forever. From that time on Judaism was a religious sect and nothing more. The scribes were the leaders, and ruled their fellow-believers; their schools were the governing bodies. Now the Talmudic writers, by a grave anachronism, transfer this conception to ancient times also. If we are to believe them, the whole history of the nation consisted chiefly in religious and juristical controversies, and the nation was divided into two religious parties or schools. Much light has been thrown upon this subject by Wellhausen's monograph *Die Pharisäer und die Sadducäer*, 1874, and by Kuenen, "Over de samenstelling van het Sanhedrin" (Verslagen en Meded. d. Kon. Akad., 1866).

After the exile Judea was a dependency successively of Persia, Egypt, and Syria. But under a provincial governor they enjoyed a relative independence. The High Priest presided over a council of elders, γερουσία, συνέδριον. Scribes did not sit in this council, at least not as such. They did not form at first a separate class or party. Originally priests and sopherim were identical, of one mind; and many priests were, like Ezra, at the same time scribes. But it was not necessary to be a priest in order to be a scribe (scripturist). Things then took this course: Gradually the dominant sacerdotal order became the class of the "*satisfaits.*" They formed the aristocracy and had no reason to look for a happier time to come. The people, on the contrary, and the scribes, who had not the largest share of the good things of the earth, or were not satisfied with them, lived in their thoughts more in the blessed future predicted by the prophets. The separation became more manifest with the progress of time, and the Pharisees (from פרש, separate; הנבדלים, Ezra 6, 12. 10, 11. Neh. 9, 2. 10, 29.) separated themselves from the worldly priestly nobility, who haughtily appealed to their descent from Zadok and called themselves Sadducees.

b. THE CANONIZATION OF THE PROPHETS.

But the division was not at once manifest; in the first two centuries after Nehemiah the difference did not come so plainly to light. Moreover, the scribes themselves, by their legal attitude, played into the hands of the hierarchy. They taught the people faithfully and willingly to pay their tithes even of mint and cummin, and this was well-pleasing to the priests. There were also among the priests in the first period men like the High Priest, Simeon II, the Just, who certainly differed very little from the scribes in tendency.

No one, therefore, in this period, thought of disputing the right of the scribes to determine what books should or should not be read in the synagogue. We must not, however, in this period identify priests and scribes. Although there was no conflict, there was a profound difference, which later developed into conflict. Ezra himself had opponents among the priests, and many certainly submitted unwillingly. Josephus says: "The Sadducees are the men of highest rank, but they have as good as no influence, for in matters of government they are forced against their will to follow the prescriptions of the Pharisees; otherwise the people would no longer tolerate them" (*Antt. Jud.* xviii. 1, 4). This was the state of things in Josephus' days, but to a greater or less extent it had always been so. The side from which all religious action originated was the Pharisæan, and to this side the scribes were addicted.

Since, however, in the first period after Nehemiah the difference had not become an open conflict, we cannot speak of a Sadducean, in contrast to a Pharisæan, Canon. The church fathers Tertullian, *De præscr. hæret.* c. 45, Origen, *Contra Celsum,* i. 11, 1, Jerome on Matt. 22, 31 f.; [*Opp.* ed. Vallarsi, VII. 179] speak of such a Canon; but these statements rest upon a misunderstanding. Josephus, who more than once sets forth at length the differences between Pharisees and Sadducees (*e. g.,* *Antt. Jud.* xiii. 10, 6; xviii. 1, 4) tells us nothing about a difference on this point. It was probably an inference from the fact that the Sadducees rejected the Pharisæan Halacha, and that the Nebiim and Kethubim were also regarded as tradition by the side of the Tora. In addition, it may have been inferred from Jesus' argument for the resurrection against the Sadducees, in Math. 22, 23—32. The fact that the Lord there cites a passage from the Law was, it was thought, because the Sadducees would not have recognized an appeal to Nebiim or Kethubim as valid. But it is forgotten that for all Jews the Law was *the* revelation, and that Jesus found the great principle of life in communion with God as a condition of the resurrection best expressed in the words which he quotes from the Tora.

But how, then, could the Sadducees deny the resurrection in view of such passages as Is. 25, 8. 26, 19; and, in case they accepted Daniel also, of Daniel 12, 2. 3? Because their recognition of these books was nothing more than a concession to the pressure of the scribes. And if they thought it worth the trouble, they doubtless had a Sadducean exegesis to get rid of these passages. Cheyne rightly remark (*Origin and religious contents of the Psalter*, London, 1891, p. 417): "The Sadducees were not, of course, opposed either to the psalms or to the prophecies.; the Sadducean author of I Maccabees evidently loved them both. But as practical men the Sadducees considered that vague poetic expressions should not be treated as *dicta probantia* for doctrine, and in particular were slow to accept even the earliest and best of apocalypses as in the fullest sense a holy book."

As for the Essenes, they certainly rejected no part of the Canon, but seem to have added to it other writings for their own edification. That they did not possess the Priestly Law, as Hilgenfeld, *Judenthum und Judenchristenthum*, p. 116, supposes, is unproved. But it is probable that they had introduced alterations into their Tora, so that it differed from that of the orthodox Jews. See in regard to them Cheyne, *l. s. c.*, *p.* 417 f., and for information as to Pharisees, Sadducees, and Essenes, Schürer, *Geschichte d. Jüd. Volkes*, II. p. 314 ff., 467 ff., *Hist. of the Jewish People*, 2d Div. vol. II. p. 1 ff., 188 ff.

¹¹ The spirit which the Canon of the Old Testament breathes is that of the scribes. This is true of the whole Canon. The overwhelmingly Sadducean Sanhedrin would certainly never have admitted, even to the third division, a book like Daniel, so intensely national, so eschatological, and so positively teaching the resurrection of the dead. A book like Ecclesiastes, however, the sopherim received only with reluctance, and even Akiba frankly admits that they had had doubts concerning it.

Another proof that the canonization was the work of the scribes, is the following. It was the sopherim who in later times disputed as to the authority of some books. The presumption is, therefore, that it was the sopherim also, who had previously decided in regard to the disputed books and others.

¹² The אנשי כנסת הגדולה are mentioned in the Mishna once (*Aboth* i. 1, 2), in the Gemaras and in the Midrash many times. The work of canonization is by many attributed to them, in conjunction with Ezra. While in *Baba bathra* fol. 15a only the "writing" of Ezekiel, the Twelve Minor Prophets, and Esther is ascribed to them, it has been said since Elias Levita, that Ezra, with the men of the Great Synagogue, fixed the Canon. In most passages of the Talmud, it is a college of one hundred and twenty persons (sometimes also of eighty five;—e. g. eighty five elders are zealous for the introduction of the feast of Purim, *Jerus. Megilla*, i. 4 (7), fol. 70, Schwab, VI. p. 206; cf. § 6, n. 6), men proficient in the Scriptures. This college is supposed to have stood, after the exile, at the head of the state. Ezra was its president, if not its founder.—The statements in regard to the Great Synagogue are confused. In its number are included Joshua, Zerubbabel, Haggai, Zechariah;

Daniel also and his companions. It is thus carried back eighty years, more or less, before Ezra. But Nehemiah, Malachi, and Mordecai, also belonged to it. It comes further down to Simeon the Just, of whom it is said (Aboth i. 2), היה מִשִּׁירֵי כנסת הגדולה (he belonged to the survivors of the Great Synagogue), and who probably lived about 200 B. C. Sometimes it is said that it was a permanent institution; sometimes that it lasted a hundred years. In any case, the ideas about it are indefinite. But the mediaeval Jewish scholars universally assumed, on the basis of these notices, that such a governing body had stood at the head of the Jewish people since the days of Ezra, and they were inclined to attribute to this college very great influence in religious matters.

In Holland, in spite of the authority of the Jewish scholars and of Joh. Buxtorf, the existence of this body has always been doubted; for example by Alting, Burman, Camp. Vitringa, Witsius. Very negative were the results of J. E. Rau (Professor at Herborn) in his *Diatribe de Synagoga Magna*, 1726. But since Jewish writers (Graetz, *Kohélet*, p. 155 ff., Bloch, *Studien*, p. 99—132, and others) had in recent times again attempted to vindicate the existence and the extended work of this assembly, Prof. Kuenen in his paper, "Over de mannen der Groote Synagoge," in *Verslagen en Mededeelingen v. d. Kon. Acad.*, Deel vi. 2e Reeks, 1876,) subjected the question again to his criticism, and proved irrefutably that the Great Synagogue belongs to the realm of legend. See a brief notice by Kuenen himself in *Theol. Tijdschrift*, 1877, p. 237 ff.

We observe here again that the Jewish scholars after the fall of Jerusalem had an entirely false idea of the older times. Israel was not ruled by the scribes before the year 70 A. D. What are we to imagine under the name Great Synagogue? A senate? Certainly not; it is supposed to have been a religious body. Kuenen, now, believes that the whole legend is based upon the narrative in Neh. 8—10. Many traces of this are preserved in the Talmudic accounts. Even the number eighty five agrees with the eighty four signers of the covenant (Neh. 10). We need only count Ezra in addition, or suppose that one name has fallen out (the Peshitto has in vs. 4 an additional Shephatia, and in vs. 10 (A. V. vs. 9) a ו stands before ישוע, so that perhaps a name has fallen out there).

If now it be assumed that the historical basis of the legend is the assembly in Neh. 8—10, then we cannot attribute to it the rôle ascribed to it by tradition. For this assembly did not legislate, but adopted a legislation. "The Talmudic great *Keneseth* is an unhistorical conception, a transformation of the assembly which under Ezra and Nehemiah adopted the complete Mosaic law book." In later times a prolonged existence came to be attributed to this assembly, because the sopherim antedated the domination of their predecessors. But the solitary passage of the Mishna (*Aboth*, i. 1. 2) probably does not do this. It is true that Simeon the Just is there counted among the "survivors of the Great Synagogue," but it must be remembered that according to the Talmudic chronology (which must here be our guide) Simeon was a contemporary of Alexander the Great, and that it reduces the entire Persian period to only fifty two years. The view that the men of the Great Synagogue were contemporaries of Ezra and formed only a single generation, has maintained itself in spite of the representation of the mediaeval Jewish scholars. In Elias Levita himself, and in R. Azariah [de Rossi] *Imre Bina*, c. 22 [ed. Wilna, 1866, p. 245] it still appears (see Wellhausen, *Einleitung*[4], p. 558, n. 1.)

We put, therefore, in place of the men of the Great Synagogue, *the older scribes*. The latter really accomplished what is ascribed to the former. They constituted no governing assembly, but were some of them priests, others not; some members of the Sanhedrin, others outside of that body. (See also W. Robertson Smith, *Old Testament in the Jewish Church*, 2 ed. p. 169, n. 1.)

---

4. As regards the method pursued by the scribes in the collection of other Holy Scriptures besides the Tora, we may lay it down, 1. that they worked in the spirit of legalism, but that the older scribes were more liberal than the later [13]. 2. That they not only brought together existing collections of prophetic writings, but themselves compiled such collections, their work thus coinciding with that of redaction [14]. 3. That in this redaction they also treated the text freely [15], although this freedom did not go to the length of readily admitting to the text haggadic additions [16].

[13] With the spirit in which they worked we have already become acquainted in § 8. But we must add that the older scribes were not as narrow as the later ones. Otherwise they would never have received such a book as Ezekiel. In later times men, not unnaturally, wondered that they had done so, and sought for an explanation of the fact.

[14] That the scribes themselves also compiled collections of prophecies is conclusively evident from the Dodekapropheton. These writings were too small to be preserved separately, and together they constituted one book which could fitly take its place by the side of the three great prophets, Isaiah, Jeremiah, and Ezekiel. The arrangement in all probability follows a chronological order, as the scribes conceived it. They closed

with Malachi, not so much because they knew that this anonymous prophet (for Malachi is not a proper name) was exactly the last, but because the end of his book, where he predicts the return of Elijah the Tishbite to prepare for the Messianic kingdom, formed a suitable conclusion for the *Nebiim Acharonim*. (c. f. § 1, n. 10).

Perhaps before Malachi was subjoined, the anonymous prophecy, Zech. 9—14, formed the conclusion of the book of the Minor Prophets. Ewald, *Propheten*[2] &c., I. p. 81, *Prophets*, I. p. 99f., has rightly observed that the titles of Zech. 12, 1 and Mal. 1, 1 are by the same hand, and are merely copies of Zech. 9, 1. In all three passages we meet the strange combination of words, משא דבר יהוה.

The question is whether other collections also were made up by them, for instance those of the Isaian prophecies and of Jeremiah's oracles. So far as Isaiah is concerned, Jesus ben Sirach already knew Isaiah as the prophet "who comforted the mourners in Zion" (Ecclus. 48, 22—25). This was about 200 B. C. But when were the collections, Is. 1—39 and 40—66, united? That Is. 1—39 had previously a separate existence is sufficiently clear from the historical chapters, which were originally placed at the end of the book, just as Jer. 52 is, to throw light upon the whole. But we do not know when the oracles of the "Great Unknown" were united to these. Fürst, *Kanon*, p. 15 ff. thinks he discovers in the statement of *Baba bathra* 14 b. a dim reminiscence of the fact that Isaiah I (1—39) and Isaiah II (40—66) were originally separate, because it is said there of Isaiah that the whole was a book of consolation, which can only be meant of ch. 40—66. The oldest order must then, in his opinion, have been: Isaiah I, Jeremiah, Ezekiel, Isaiah II. But he finds too much in the words. Once regarded as a whole, the last chapters of Isaiah stand out so prominently that the whole book might very well be called a book of consolation. The collection Ch. 1—39 also can hardly have been edited in this form by Isaiah himself. Chapter 20, dated in the year of the capture of Ashdod by a general of Sargon's (711 B. C.), should properly come after Ch. 28, which presumes that the Northern Kingdom still exists. The strange position of the vision of Isaiah's call, in Ch. 6 instead of Ch. 1, may be due to the prophet himself, who thought it best to make the vision known only when he came to publish a second collection of prophecies. What later Jewish scholars thought about the composition of the Isaian collection and about the incorporation in it of certain small prophecies is very interesting, but of no importance for our enquiry (see Fürst, *l. c.* p. 26. 27).

As to Jeremiah, the LXX presents a text that is exempt from some of the glosses and interpolations which have injured the Massoretic text. (See e. g. on Jer. 27, W. Robertson Smith, *Old Testament in Jewish Church*, 2 ed. p. 103 ff.) But we now confine our attention to the redaction. It at once attracts our notice that the prophecies against the heathen occupy a different position in the Greek translation from that which they have in the Hebrew Bible. In the latter they stand at the end, Ch. 46—51. In the LXX they come after Ch. 25, 13, and the words of this verse thus form the title, instead of Ch. 46, 1. This may indeed have been an intentional alteration; but it may quite as well have been so in the original. In either case it proves the freedom exercised in the redaction. (On the history of the Book of Jeremiah, see Prof. Valeton Jr., *Viertal Voorlezingen over Profeten des O. V*, 1886, p. 96, n. 1; *Letterkunde des O. V.* § 13.)

The recognition of the fact that the post-exilic scribes, who have transmitted to us the prophetic literature of the Old Testament, also selected and worked over this literature, necessarily brings with it the obligation to take account of the fact in interpreting these writings. Not only does the authenticity of the titles thus become disputable, so that the author's authority cannot be alleged for the order of the divisions and subdivisions, but it must further be admitted that material changes also may be laid to the account of these sopherim. The discussion of all this would, however, lead us too far. See Kuenen, *H. C. O.*², II. p. 20—25. We will only add the remark that the redaction of the Hexateuch also (§ 9, n. 4), and the final redaction of the historical books, must be attributed to the earliest scribes. Cf. § 10, 1, remembering that for them collection was equivalent to redaction.

15 That in the earliest period of canonization the text of the Old Testament was treated with freedom, can in our day hardly be any longer gainsaid. But this is not the place to prove it in extenso. It must suffice here to recall the fact that the Jewish scholars themselves have preserved the memory of it. The Men of the Great Synagogue are said to have replaced indecent expressions by more becoming ones. (*Tanchuma*, fol. 26*a*; see J. S. Bloch, *Studien, u. s. w.*, p. 123). They also enumerate five omissions of the scribes, עִטּוּרֵי סוֹפְרִים, and (usually) eighteen emendations of the scribes, תִּקּוּנֵי סוֹפְרִים, which may be seen in *Ochla W'ochla*, ed. Dr. S. Frensdorff, Hannover, 1864, No. 217 and 168. The purpose of these corrections is almost always to remove offenses of one kind or another. These twenty three alterations may, indeed, be adduced as a proof of the faithful transmission of the text, it being said that the sopherim have so scrupulously preserved the Scriptures, that they record every alteration which they made. But the attentive scrutiny of the text and comparison with the LXX teaches something altogether different. Dr. Abr. Geiger is, therefore, most certainly right when he regards the twenty three alterations specified as but a few specimens of what the scribes ventured to do. In his *Urschrift und Uebersetzungen der Bibel*, he goes through the entire Old Testament, and points out many

passages where in his opinion the tikkun sopherim has replaced the original (p. 308 ff.); and though he greatly exaggerates, in principle he is right. See further Wellhausen, *Einleitung*⁴, p. 624 ff.

[16] However freely the earlier scribes handled the text, they never allowed haggadic additions, like those which are found, for example, in Daniel and Esther in the LXX, to be received into the text. They were certainly delivered orally in the synagogue; for it is not to be assumed that they are all of Egyptian origin. The additions to the book of Esther, which, according to the subscription, Lysimachus ben Ptolemaeus of Jerusalem translated into Greek, were probably also appended to the book by him. But they were not received into Hebrew manuscripts. (See Oort, *Laatste Eeuwen*, I. p. 191 ff.; and cf. further as to passages which have perhaps made their way into the Old Testament from a Midrash, Budde, *Z. A. W.*, 1892, p. 37 ff.)

§ 11.

HISTORY OF THE COLLECTION OF THE OLD TESTAMENT BOOKS, CONTINUED.

c. THE CANONIZATION OF THE "WRITINGS" AND CLOSE OF THE CANON OF THE OLD TESTAMENT.

Direct historical statements about the third collection of the Old Testament Scriptures are wanting, as in the case of the second. Nevertheless, in the light of the historical evidence, we are able to give to the following questions an answer that agrees with well established facts: 1. When was the foundation laid for this collection? 2. What course and method was followed in forming it? 3. What state had it reached in the first century of our era? 4. When may the collection of the Hagiographa be regarded as finally fixed?

1. The foundation of the collection of the Kethubim is formed by the first and most important book in it, the Book of Psalms. Nehemiah himself added an earliest collection of Davidic poems to the series of prophetic writings and other documents which he preserved in the temple (2 Macc. 2, 13)[1]. To this other writings were gradually added.

[1] See § 4, n. 6 and § 10, n. 2. It is remarkable that this passage has never exerted any influence upon Jewish opinions. Jewish scholars are still unable to perceive its importance; witness Graetz (*Kohélet*, p. 151, 152), Bloch (*Studien, u. s. w., p.* 62 f.), and Geiger (*Nachgelassene Schriften*, IV. p. 16 f.). With what right we appeal to 2 Macc. 2, 13, we have shown in § 4, n: 6. What can be meant by τὰ τοῦ Δαυίδ? The whole Psalter? This is not probable. It was formerly thought possible to deny the existence of Maccabaean Psalms, among other reasons, because the Canon was already fixed in the days of Nehemiah. This argument is now out of date. But does not 2 Macc. 2, 13 prove the same thing? It appears to us that we must ascribe to the phrase τὰ τοῦ Δαυίδ a more limited sense; and this not only on account of our own view of the history of the formation of the Psalter, which we cannot more

the Tora, probably occurs even as late as *Megilla* iii. 1; from which passage we may infer that in the Teba (the chest for sacred scriptures in the synagogue), at least in earlier times,* were kept the Tora and the Sepharim (including the five Megilloth). For we find enumerated, a place of prayer (רחובה), a synagogue (בית הכנסת), a box or chest (תיבה), a cover or cloth in which to wrap up the rolls (מטפחת), holy writings (ספרים), and a roll of the Tora (תורה). According to this Mishna, the price received from the sale of any one of these may be used to buy that which next follows it in the series, but not vice versa; the series being repeated in inverse order, — Tora roll, scriptures, cover, chest, synagogue, open place of, prayer (cf. § 8, n. 4). It is clear that the author of this Mishna has in mind a synagogue, and he ascends from the lowest, the external, to the higher; from the house of prayer to the Teba, then successively to what is contained in the Teba, &c. The word Sepharim also maintained itself as a specific name for that part which was first made canonical (Prophets), as we have seen from Dan. 9, 2.

But when once a division had been made in the collection which had originally been one, τὰ λοιπὰ τῶν βιβλίων (Prologue to Sirach) could not equally well be called Sepharim. In its place there came into use the word כתובים, which in classical Hebrew does not occur as a substantive, but only as a passive participle (Jos. 8, 34. 10, 13. and even as late as 1 Chron. 29, 29). In this way the name Kethubim and the terms employed in the Prologue to Sirach are best explained.

---

* This passage from the Mishna gives only indirect evidence that in earlier times other sacred books also were kept in the Teba. But Tertullian (*de cultu femin.*, i. 3) seems to confirm the existence of this older practise, when he says of the book of Enoch, "nec in armarium Judaicum dmittitur." (Quoted by Buhl, *Kanon*, Engl. trans. p. 41, cf. above § 8, n. 2).

Light is, moreover, thrown by this theory upon the statement of Jerome (§ 7, n. 3), that there were some in his day who would place Ruth and Lamentations in the third section, while he himself counts them among the Prophets. That the transfer of Ruth and Lamentations to the third section did not take place until the 3d or 4th century A. D. (Kuenen, *H. K. O.*^{1}, III. p. 446), is a large conclusion to draw from Jerome's statement; see § 1, n. 12. The Jewish accounts know nothing of it, and according to the Preface to his translation of Daniel (see Buhl, *Kanon*, p. 20; Engl. transl., p. 20) Jerome was aware, at least after he wrote the *Prologus galeatus*, that the enumeration of eight books of the Nebiim and eleven of the Kethubim was the usual one among the Jews. Still, this statement of Jerome and that of Origen (§ 7, n. 2) are not entirely without significance. Our theory does justice to this, and to the order of the LXX. Before the division into Prophets and the "rest of the books", Ruth was probably generally placed after Judges, and Lamentations after Jeremiah. When the division was made, these books could not be considered as belonging to the Prophets, and hence were counted among "the rest." This was the official theory. But many may have included these little appendices, and perhaps others also, in their copies of the Prophets, which were more likely to be in the possession of private individuals than copies of the Kethubim. It must never be forgotten that the Canon was a theory, and not an edition of the text.*

---

* At what time the Jews began to unite all the Holy Scriptures in a single manuscript it is impossible to say with certainty. Perhaps as early as the second century A. D., or the close of the first century; at least deliverances on the question whether all the sacred books may be united in one manuscript or not, have been transmitted to us from teachers of the second and of the end of the first century; see *Baba bathra* fol. 13b where we

Manuscripts of the Prophets from the period before 200 B. C. may have existed, and been frequently transcribed, in which Ruth and Lamentations were regularly included. To this the scribes themselves could have no objections, since these books also were held in high esteem, and the practice did not affect the theory, which always counted them among the Kethubim.

3 In enumerating by name those books of the Kethubim, which in our opinion were already in existence when the Prophets were declared to be Sacred Scripture, we pass into the field of special introduction; but it will be perceived that this in no way affects our main result. In the third century B. C. there were in existence, a great part of the Psalms, the books of Job, Ruth, Lamentations, Proverbs, Canticles; about 250 B. C. appeared the work of the Chronicler, originally a single whole, Chronicles-Ezra-Nehemiah (cf. 2 Chron. 36, 23 with Ezra 1, 1 f; and see further the various O. T. Introductions). Most of these books were held in high esteem. But the work of the Chronicler can hardly at first have been placed on an equality with the others;

---

read as follows: "Our teachers declared it permissible to have Tora, Nebiim, and Kethubim united in one manuscript. This was the teaching of R. Meïr [2d century]; whereas R. Judah [ben Ilai] affirmed: the Law by itself, the Prophets by themselves, and the Writings by themselves. The learned held, Each book must be by itself. R. Judah related an instance; Boethus b. Zunim had the eight books of the Prophets united in one manuscript, which Eleazar ben Azariah [end of the 1st century] approved; there were others, however, who said, It was not so, but he had each book separate. Rabbi [i. e. R. Judah the Holy] said, A copy was brought to us which contained Tora, Nebiim, and Kethubim united, and we sanctioned it." See Wünsche, *Der babylonische Talmud in seinen haggad. Bestandtheilen übersetzt*, 2ter. Halbband, 2te Abth., p. 136 f.; cf., *Jerus. Megilla*, iii. 1., fol. 73d.; *Massechet Sopherim*, iii. 1 ff. p. V. (Buhl, *Kanon*, p. 40, 98; Engl. trans., 41, 196 f.). For use in synagogues, however, such manuscripts were never permitted. For this purpose separate rolls are required.

it was too recent for that. Even at a later time, it was only put among the Kethubim Acharonim, with the still more recent book of Daniel (cf. § 11, n. 14). But it should be remembered that the work of the Chronicler, however much it differed from Samuel and Kings, was not entirely new. The Chronicler had predecessors of the same turn of mind. Among his sources he mentions a midrash of the Books of Kings (2 Chron. 24, 27 ; see Kuenen *H. C. O.*², I. p. 486 f.); and he gave a last reworking of the history in the priestly spirit, so that his work need not have produced any surprise among his contemporaries.

4 We regard the books of Ecclesiastes, Esther, and Daniel as younger than the 3d. century B. C. (see *Letterkunde des O. V.*, § 26, 27). But it should be again observed that our main argument does not in the least depend upon this opinion. We have said in the text, "Books written later *could* be received into it." If anyone be disposed to regard these books as older than most investigators in the Old Testament field do, it can in no way alter our result.

5 The statements of the text need no demonstration. We shall return to Ecclesiastes and Esther. A single word only in regard to Job and Daniel. The Jewish scholars thought that the book of Job was written by Moses (*Baba bathra* fol. 14*b*, 15*a*), probably in accordance with the doctrine, taught by Josephus also, that every prophet described his own period, and Job was believed to have lived in the time of the patriarchs (see § 6, n. 3). But if the book was not received because Moses was believed to be its author, it obtained a place because it treated of a famous personage of antiquity (Ezek. 14, 14). At least that was the formal requirement of which the book had to correspond. It is to the credit of the scribes that they included this important work. In the same way, they were strongly inclined to receive the book of Daniel (written about 165 B. C.) for the sake of its contents. And there was no formal difficulty

in the way of doing so, since it was believed to have been written by the celebrated Daniel, famous in the exile, which made him for the Jews of the 1st century B. C. a man of ancient times.

---

3. For Christian theologians the question what the state of the canon of the Old Testament was in the first century of our era is of sufficient importance to deserve separate consideration. At that time the Law had already enjoyed canonical authority for about five centuries, the Prophets for more than two centuries, and the division of the "Writings" was, according to the prevailing opinion, reckoned to have substantially the same compass as it has in our Bibles [6]. But no authoritative decision had yet been delivered concerning this third collection. It is also very questionable whether the Galilean synagogues, especially in small places, possessed all the Kethubim; and we may safely assume that such books as Ecclesiastes, Canticles, and Esther were not much read by humble devout persons for their own edification; though they never thought of antagonizing the scribes, who gave there books a place of honour by the side of the Law, and the Prophets, and the Psalms [7].

[6] We infer this from the testimony of Josephus and 4 (2)Esdras; but see further on in this paragraph.

c. THE CANONIZATION OF THE "WRITINGS."

7 All we can say with certainty is that, in the days of Jesus and the Apostles, the Law and the Prophets were read in the synagogues. This was done even then, so far as the Law is concerned, in accordance with fixed rules; see § 1, n. 7, and § 5.

We know nothing with certainty about any reading from the "Writings" in those days. It may, however, be believed that this was done, although special days were never fixed for it, as for the Megilloth. Such books as the Psalms and Daniel were certainly much read. We know also that selections from Job, Ezra, or Chronicles, or from Daniel were read before the High Priest on the night before the Great Day of Atonement (see, for instance, Oort, *Theol. Tijdschrift*, 1876, p. 147), — a proof, certainly, of the high esteem in which these writings were held. But poor synagogues did not allow themselves the luxury of buying all the "Writings." Even in our own day, a synagogue is sufficiently equipped, if, in addition to the five rolls of the Tora, it possesses the five Megilloth. The haphtaras from the Prophets may be read from a prayer-book.

We can also be well assured that in the circles of the humble devout from which the Saviour chose his most faithful disciples such writings as Ecclesiastes, Canticles, and Esther were little read. Whether they might be permitted in the synagogue or not, was a question with which they did not concern themselves. All that the scribes and Pharisees taught, sitting in Moses' seat, they observed and did (Matt. 23, 2. 3). But their spiritual life depended upon no decision of the ecclesiastical authorities. They read Ecclesiastes, Canticles, and Esther very little. While the N. T. exhibits numerous traces of acquaintance with apocrypha, the books named are nowhere quoted. The allegorical interpretation of Canticles, which first appears in 4(2) Esdras 5, 24. 26. 7, 26 and is also defended in the Talmud (Fürst, *Kanon*, p. 84 f.), was, therefore, at that time probably not general, while the book itself was not universally received in the synagogue. In regard to Ecclesiastes and Esther, also, the learned leaders were not yet altogether of one mind. We need not therefore be surprised, or regard it as an accident, that from just the books of Ecclesiastes, Canticles, and Esther no quotations occur in the New Testament (see § 5, n. 4, and § 7, n. 1.)

---

4. For the fixing of the number of books in the Kethubim, and thus at the same time for the close of the Old Testament Canon, we can give no other certain date than a *terminus ad quem*, the redaction of the Mishna by Rabbi Judah the Holy (about 200 A. D.). This work, of course, presupposes a fixed Canon of Holy Scripture [8]. At that time the last objections were silenced. But already in the first century of our era an opinion established itself which virtually agreed with the later view; and at the close of the first century (Flav. Josephus and 4 (2) Esdras) it was as good as universal [9]. From the middle of the second century we may reckon that all scribes were agreed on the subject [10]. A more exact determination of the date cannot be given [11]. The earlier doubts were, indeed, not quite forgotten; but more and more, as time went on, the final decision was conceived to have been reached at

c. THE CANONIZATION OF THE "WRITINGS." 147

a very remote time, in the days of Ezra and the Men of the Great Synagogue [12].

For this third collection the indefinite name Kethubim was retained. The name Hagiographa comes from the Church Fathers, though it is entirely in the spirit of the Jewish theologians [13]. The division into Kethubim Rishonim and Acharonim, besides the five Megilloth, is an imitation of the division of the Nebiim; but has nevertheless some historical significance [14].

[8] After Rabbi Akiba, R. Meïr, and others had already made collections of halacha's, which, however, have been lost, Rabbi Judah hak-kadosh, performed this task (Oort, *Laatste Eeuwen*, II. p. 416; and on the Mishna of R. Akiba, Graetz, *Gesch. d. Juden*, IV. p. 57 f. and p. 430.) This work presupposes a closed Canon, and it is evident from the contents of the Mishna that its Canon is that of twenty-four books with which we are acquainted; this number is frequently mentioned. (Fürst, *Kanon d. A. T.*, p. 51.)

[9] Flavius Josephus and 4 (2) Esdras (see the passages, § 4, n. 8 and 7) prove most clearly that the number twenty four was virtually fixed about 100 A. D. Public opinion was really already settled. But it still awaited its sanction from the schools. Not a single other book applied for admission; there was only one point on which some scribes were not clear; namely, whether the number should not be reduced by the removal of Ecclesiastes, or Canticles, or Esther (§ 8, n, 2 ; Nöldeke, *die alttest. Literatur*, 1868, p. 238.)

Our conception of the course of events commends itself, and is supported by the historical facts set forth in the preceding paragraph. It still seems probable to me, even after reading Buhl's opinion on the subject (*Kanon u. Text*, p. 27). According to Buhl the third section had already found "seinen kanonischen Abschluss" before Christ; and the discussions about the disputed writings and the final settlement wear only the character of a "Revision," which must have occurred as early as toward the end of the first century A. D. I agree, indeed, with Geiger, that all these discussions were mere scholastic disputations, which to a very limited extent affected public opinion; but I also believe that the supposed "kanonischer Abschluss" had been accomplished only in this public opinion; in other words, that gradually there had been formed a *communis opinio*, and nothing more.

[10] If we take the proposed *terminus ad quem*, 200 A. D., and reflect that among those who took part in the discussions as to the sanctity of certain books R. Akiba (died 135) is mentioned, the date proposed, about 150 A. D., is certainly very close to the truth. The spirit of the age also demanded a settled Canon. Think of the exegetical work and method of Akiba, which presupposes at least a fixed Canon and equally a settled text, and of the attempt of Akiba's pupil Aquila to supersede the Greek version of the LXX by a more exact one. (See Oort, *Laatste Eeuwen*, II. p. 415 and W. Robertson Smith. *Old Testament in the Jewish Church*, 2 ed. p. 63 f. and n.) One thing more. The first Canon originated when the people of Israel, after the exile, had become a religious community. But gradually the community had again become, however imperfectly, a nation. After 70 A. D. Judaism became, through the work of Gamaliel II, for all time, a pretty close community or church. Such a community must have a Bible about whose extent there can be no dispute (cf. an article by Prof. Oort in *Theol. Tijdschrift.*, 1883, p. 560 f).

[11] Graetz is of the opinion, first expressed in his *Geschichte*

d. Juden, III. p. 355 ff.; 494—502, that an official resolution about the Canon was passed in the tumultuous assembly of the year 66 A. D., at the outbreak of the Jewish war, in which "the eighteen rules" (about the intercourse of Jews with Gentiles) were adopted. This is merely a conjecture, for which no evidence exists, but against which argue the facts, 1. that the moment for such a discussion would have been ill chosen; 2. that before A. D. 70 the scribes had not yet the power completely in their hands; 3. that this assembly is never subsequently mentioned in connection with the Canon. See the refutation of these conjectures by Kuenen *H. K. O.*^{1}, III. p. 442, n. 24. More recently Graetz has attempted to defend his position again in Anhang I of his *Kohélet*, p. 147—173. His theory is, that at the assembly of A. D. 66 Ecclesiastes was excluded through the influence of the school of Shammai. Thirty-five or forty years later, in 101 or 106, another assembly of the same kind was held under the patriarchate of Rabban Gamaliel II in Jamnia (*Eduyoth* v . 3), at which the matter was again discussed, and Ecclesiastes admitted.

It is to be noted, that Graetz makes all these guesses (for they are nothing more) in support of his hypothesis that Ecclesiastes is very recent, and a satire on king Herod the Great. But according to nearly all investigators this book is older. And if in 66 A. D. it was officially excluded (Graetz supposes that, on account of the war, the protocol of the assembly was not drawn up, and so the genuine tradition lost!), it is surely very improbable that it was received again in 101 or 106. He further (p. 47) agrees with Krochmal (died 1840), who first advanced this opinion, that the epilogue, Eccl. 12, 9—14, was written by the men of Jamnia, and was intended for the entire third section. So also Bloch, *Studien, u. s. w.*, p. 137. But see the defense of the epilogue by Kuenen, *H. C. O.*^{2}, III. p. 179 f., among others against Prof. P. de Jong, *De Prediker vertaald en verklaard*, Leiden, 1861, p. 142 f.; cf. Kuenen, *Theol. Tijdschrift*, 1883, p. 119—126; also Cheyne, *Job and Solomon*, 1887, p. 282; *Letterkunde des O. V.*, § 26, n. 7. But we need not here enter upon this isagogic question. The assertion of Graetz and Bloch is refuted by the fact that it was precisely on account of the closing words that the book was deemed worthy of adoption (see § 6, n. 5 and § 7, n. 4; and Fürst, *Kanon*, p. 93). Hence, even if it be thought that the epilogue must be regarded as a later addition, we are still compelled to assume (with Cheyne, for instance, *Job and Solomon*, p. 282) that the addition had taken place long before the definitive adoption into the Canon, and before the book was in esteem as a religious work. (Cf. also Cheyne, *Job and Solomon*, p. 232 f.)

Wellhausen also (*Einleitung* [4], p. 550 ff.) is of the opinion, that "according to a credible, although vague and fragmentary tradition of the rabbins", the Pharisean scribes, shortly after 70 A. D., definitively settled the extent of the Canon. He refers, among others to Kuenen, *H. K. O*,[1] III. p. 415, whom he manifestly takes to affirm more than that scholar really does, and to the important work of J. Derenbourg, *Essai sur l'histoire et la géographie de la Palestine d'après les Thalmuds et les autres sources rabbiniques*, Paris, 1867, p. 295. But Derenbourg adduces no proofs, and obviously has in mind the ingenious hypothesis of Graetz.

[12] The notices in the Gemaras prove that the objections were not forgotten. That they were still *felt* is shown by *Megilla* fol. 7a (see § 6, n. 6), where the objection against Esther is brought up by R. Samuel, who lived in the 3d century A. D. (Bloch, *Studien, u. s. w.*, p. 153). But ever more and more the final decision was thought of as falling in remote antiquity. So in *Aboth de R. Nathan* c. i, where the decision in regard to Canticles, Ecclesiastes and Proverbs is attributed to the Men of the Great Synagogue (see § 6, n. 4).

c. THE CANONIZATION OF THE "WRITINGS."

¹³ The general appellation "Writings" did not need to be changed, because in the collection of this third group there was originally not the least intention of putting a Canon of similar rank by the side of the Law and the Prophets. It did not occur to any one, for instance, to have them publicly read by pericopes. The object was to preserve these writings from profanation. They were indeed read in the synagogue, but it is plain that often little respect was shown them; and it was this particularly that the scribes wished to guard against (Graetz, *Kohélet*, p. 162). The dogmatic theory of the church Fathers led to the translation of the word כתובים not by γραφεῖα but by ἁγιόγραφα. But in this they were in complete accord with the Jewish scholars, who held all these writings to have been inspired by the Holy Ghost (Fürst, *Kanon*, p. 55). Did the name כתבי הקדש also give occasion to this? According to Geiger, *Nachgelassene Schriften*, IV. 1876, p. 12, it is altogether incorrect to identify this expression with כתובים קדושים; it means nothing but *Writings of Israel*; הקדש (the sanctuary) is in fact in the later usage a standing appellation for Israel.

¹⁴ On the various arrangements of the books in the Talmud and Massora, see Kuenen *H. K. O.*¹, III. *p*. 448, Fürst, *Kanon*, *p*. 59, and Buhl, *Kanon u. Text*, *p*. 39, Engl. trans. p. 39 f. As at an earlier time, after the Davidic group of Psalms had been enlarged by the addition of the Levitical collections (Korahite, Elohistic), the Psalter was divided, probably after the pattern of the Tora, into five books, so now the pattern of the Nebiim was followed for the Kethubim as a whole, and they were divided into *Rishonim* and *Acharonim*. The five Megilloth were placed by themselves in the middle (in the order of the festivals at which they were read)*; or Ruth was connected with Psalms, and Ecclesiastes with Proverbs, so

---

* [In German manuscripts.]

that these books belong to the Kethubim Rishonim, while Esther as a historical book was often reckoned among the Kethubim Acharonim (cf. § 1, n. 8). It is noteworthy that the Kethubim Rishonim contain, generally speaking, the oldest books, or at least books of which a considerable part is old; while the Kethubim Acharonim — and this can hardly be accidental — contain later books, Daniel, Ezra-Nehemiah-Chronicles.

The only other thing which may seem strange is that, while Ezra-Nehemiah originally formed one historical work with Chronicles, they have not only been divided, but Chronicles is placed last. The most probable explanation is, that of this great work only Ezra-Nehemiah was originally included in the Canon, the contents of Chronicles being entirely parallel to Samuel and Kings; and that it was not until later that a place began to be made for Chronicles also. (See Kuenen *H. C. O.*², I. p. 515, n. 3). The later adoption of Chronicles into the Canon can not be inferred from the mere fact that it is put last in the series of books; for this is merely a theoretical order (though it may rest upon the late adoption), and according to another theory, preserved especially in the Spanish manuscripts and purporting to be the Palestinian order (see § 1, n. 10, 11, 12), Chronicles in turn stands first in the list of the Hagiographa. Our opinion, accordingly, is chiefly based on the fact that the original work, comprising Chronicles, Ezra and Nehemiah, is divided, and so completely separated that the first part comes (in the Talmudic arrangement followed by German manuscripts and printed editions) to stand at the end, after Ezra and Nehemiah, or (in Spanish manuscripts) as first of the whole series of Writings, while Ezra and Nehemiah come quite at the end. Thus it is quite possible that the theory in accordance with which Chronicles is put latest in order is a consequence of its late adoption. (Against Buhl, *Kanon und Text*, p. 39, Engl. transl. p. 39 f.)

§ 12.

CONCLUSION.

Our enquiry into the origin of the Old Testament Canon has led us, on the one hand, to negative results regarding the traditional views adopted from the Jews in the 16th century [1]; but, on the other hand, it has yielded us important positive results by exhibiting to us the history of the canonization of the Old Testament Scriptures in its true form; while at the same time it enables us to understand how the Christian church can, in the main, accept without difficulty the Jewish Canon [2].

[1] In view of all that has already been said, this needs no further demonstration. We only remind our readers here that it was impossible that Jesus should acknowledge the Old Testament Canon as such, although in His days about the same books were, no doubt, accounted to belong to the Holy Scriptures as are found in our own Old Testament. But what a misconception of Jesus' person and teaching comes out in the idea that the Saviour felt himself bound to a Canon! A Canon grows up only when men have become conscious that the word of prophecy is silent forever, and has significance only for those who, now that they can no more hear it, would read over the word of the Lord spoken in times past. Have men never read, "He taught as one having

§ 12. CONCLUSION.

authority and not as the scribes"? (Matt. 7, 29.) Certainly the O. T. had for the Lord great importance. He read it and lived it. In the history of God's kingdom in Israel he saw the foreshadowing of his own life; the law in the Kingdom of God, through suffering to glory, through death to life, He, who was the fulfilment of all longings and promises, recognized as the law of his own life. But did he need for this the sanction of synagogue and scribes? He, who understood the ways and purposes of God as no one before or after Him ever did, who heard God's voice as no one else ever heard it, — He saw the counsel of God reveal itself in the history of His people, in the words of His prophets, He read the books of the Old Covenant with an insight which the vindicators of the letter and the disputants about the Canon did not possess. But enough; the notion that *the* Prophet, the Revelation of God by preeminence, deemed Himself bound by a Canon can only arise in a heart so ignorant of the whole nature of scientific criticism, and therefore so afraid of it, that it will rather admit a gross inconsistency in its conception of the Saviour than let go its cherished tradition.

2 It is the two points mentioned which we wish to set forth more fully in the remainder of this paragraph. We shall make clear the true significance of the history of Canonization, and then explain why the Christian church can in the main adopt the Canon of the Jews.

The prime cause of the canonization of the Old Testament books was the constraining impulse of piety to live in accordance with the will of Yahwé as He had revealed his will through His prophets. For this reason, before the exile, prince and people bound themselves to live according to the Law of Deuteronomy, and Israel after the exile subjected itself to the Law which Ezra brought with him from Babylon [3].

But though the demands of Yahwé as interpreted by the prophets were put in force in the Law, these demands included much more than could be embodied in the Tora. The devout people continued, therefore, to read the prophecies and prophetico-historical books; and for the scribes there could be no valid reason whatever, formal or material, why they should refuse the Nebiim a place of honour by the side of the Tora [4].

When the Prophets also were officially admitted to be read in the synagogue, there already existed other older writings, which, on account of their contents and reputed origin, were held in high esteem. Among these must be included especially the Psalms, Proverbs, and Job. They could in part claim a pre-exilic origin. But this was not the only reason why they were read by the devout with so much pleasure. The collection of Davidic poems comforted them in suffering, and many a poet felt himself impelled by them to imitate the songs of the ancient singers. Thus the Psalter, originally intended for the temple, became more and more the response of the believing community to the prophetic testimony in the Tora and Nebiim [5]. The Psalter, together with Proverbs, the book of everyday life, and Job, the book of suffering, were the nucleus about which grouped themselves other writings of greater or less importance for the true spiritual life [6].

This course of the history teaches us that it was, indeed, Jewish scribes who ultimately decided upon the extent of the Canon; but that in doing so they did not wholly follow their own judgment, but in the main only authorized what was dictated by the practical spiritual life of the devout in Israel; and the practical use could not be wholly regulated by any official decision of the synagogue authorities. Not till after the year 70 A. D. did the sopherim succeed in permanently setting their stamp upon the Jewish people [7].

[3] We cannot here discuss at length the relation of the Law and the Prophets to each other. It must suffice to remind the reader that the traditional conception, according to which the whole Mosaic Law as we have it in the Pentateuch was already in existence at the beginning of Israel's history,—a view which is now regarded by nearly all Old Testament scholars as unhistorical,—is unable rightly to explain the significance of the Prophets. It can make nothing else of these men of God than interpreters of the Tora of Moses, as, following in the footsteps of Jewish scholars, it has often done.

The more recent investigations do more justice both to the

Prophets and to the Tora. For us the prophets are not mere forerunners of the scribes; and the Law is a living idea. The history of the Mosaic Tora is, that more and more as time went on the prophetic *cachet*, that is, the attestation of Yahwé's will, was stamped upon the rules of the civil and religious life. This process was begun by Moses, the prophet to whom God spoke "mouth to mouth" (Num. 2, 8), and Ezra 9, 11 teaches us that this meaning of Tora was not yet wholly forgotten even after the exile.

Thus Deuteronomy is an attempt to give heed to the demand of the prophets who had lifted up their voices against the worship on the high places (Amos, Hosea), and at the same time to realize the idea expressed by an Isaiah, that Israel must be a holy people in Yahwé's dwelling place at Jerusalem. The Law of Ezra also attempts in its own way to accomplish this, especially in a field in which the expurgation of heathenish elements has always proved to be most difficult, namely, in the cultus. On the historical significance of the expression "Mosaic" Law see further, Prof. Valeton, Sr. in *Studiën, Theol. Tijdschrift*, Groningen, 1879, p. 173—177, and my article in *Theol. Studiën*, Utrecht, 1887, p. 243 f., 328 f., 334 f., 351 f.

It will be seen from all this that the original idea of tora, even in the post-exilic community, was very much broader than in later Judaism. This broader conception allowed of the prophetic scriptures' being held in honour as the Word of God. Only a later one-sided development of the idea of tora made it necessary to affirm with emphasis the canonical authority of the Prophets.

4 The Law is thus a temporary stagnation in Israel's spiritual development. The Law collects in a preliminary way the prophetic ideas, and casts them in moulds, but cannot include them all. The prophetic horizon is more extensive; the thoughts of the prophets have a far wider scope. But the lines could

not yet be drawn all the way; the distant vision which stood before their souls could not yet be realized; the fullness of the times was not yet come.

Hence the best part of the godly in Israel could not be satisfied with keeping and spinning out regulations, which were indeed based upon the words of the prophets, but altogether failed fully to proclaim God's counsel for redemption. They continued to read the prophets, as they had begun to do in the exile. For even thus early began that change in the religious life of Israel which was to transfer its centre from the temple to the synagogue. (See Cheyne, Commentary on Is. 56, 1—8, 3d ed., 1884, II. p. 62; cf. Oort, *Laatste Eeuwen*, II. p. 391).

Thus there arise in Irael two divergent tendencies; on the one side the devout element among the people, supported by a few scribes, who hold in honour the prophetic word in its broad, evangelical scope; and on the other side the dominant spirit of the times, which regards the formulation of the prophetic demands in the Law as all sufficient. The latter, which did not understand the significance of the Law as a $\pi\alpha\varrho\varepsilon\iota\sigma\varepsilon\lambda\vartheta\acute{o}\nu$ (Rom. 5, 20), and thus occupied a position directly opposite to the Christian view, carried the day in the Jewish schools. They could not, however, banish the Prophets, and had indeed no occasion to do so, because they read their oracles through the spectacles of their own legalism. The prophets had been interpreters of Moses' law, and were honored because they had so faithfully transmitted the oral law!

5 We have indicated in the preceding paragraph that the Psalter was the fundamental part of the third collection. This fact enables us also to define the essential significance of the O. T. Canon for us. The summary in Luke 24, 44, Law, Prophets, and Psalms, really expresses what the Canon is for us. Law and Prophets comprise what God requires of His people. Not, however, in quite the same way. While the Prophets con-

tain evangelic truth also, in the Law the demands of God appear altogether as adverse to us. But that the Old Testament church understood also those elements which were completely realized by Jesus Christ and are explaimed by the Apostle Paul, appears from the response to God's testimony which the believing community gave in the Psalter.

The answer to the question as to the authority of the Old Testament Canon belongs to Dogmatics, and is out of place in an historical enquiry. But this answer must take careful account of the historical enquiry. Not that science should dominate religious belief; but because this belief, scientifically formulated, must rest upon a correct understanding of Holy Scripture. And how are we to understand the Scripture unless we regard it first of all in the light of the historical environment in which it originated? So much would appear certain, that a dogmatic definition of the authority of the Old Testament Canon which admits no distinction in worth between the parts of the Canon, relatively to one another, or puts this whole Canon on an equality with the New Testament, shows that it has no eye for the ways of God in history with His people Israel, nor for his leadings in the history of our own times and the light which in our days is being shed upon the Old Testament.

What the prophetic judgment is as to the work and meaning of a Sacred Scripture, may be learned from Jeremiah's attitude toward the oldest Canon, the Law of Deuteronomy. See the article by Lic. K. Marti, "Das erste officielle Bekenntniss", *Zeitschr. f. Theologie u. Kirche*, 1892, p. 29 ff.

⁶ That Proverbs and Job also soon came into notice is not strange. The other books have no such great significance, and we infer from the New Testament that the devout in Israel read them little or not at all. Only Daniel and Chronicles were esteemed among them.

⁷ If it had depended upon the Jewish scribes to give us a

Canon, we should certainly not have received the precious treasure we now possess (see § 8). But as it is, while meaning to leave us only kabbala on the Law, they have in fact put in our hands the history of Yahwé's counsel with His people, which is completely realized in Jesus Christ. They thought, however, that they were handing down nothing but Tora. Therefore we read in a book of the 9th century: "The poet Asaph said (Ps. 78, 1), Give ear, my people, to my Tora, &c... Then Israel asked Asaph, Is there then another Tora, that thou sayest, Give ear, my people to my Tora? We received it [the Tora] at Sinai. He answered them, The wicked in Israel say that the Nebiim and Kethubim are not Tora; but we do not believe them, for it is said, We did not hearken to the voice of Yahwé our God, to walk in his toroth which he set before us through his servants the prophets (Dan. 9, 10). Therefore the Nebiim and the Kethubim are Tora, for it is said [also], Give ear, my people, to my Tora (Ps. 78, 1)." (*Tanchuma* on Deut., Par. Re'eh. i, ed. Buber, fol. 10a; Fürst, *Kanon*, p. 51). Before the year 70 the scribes were not able permanently to set their stamp upon the spiritual life of the people. For on the one side those who were inclined toward Sadduceism eluded them, and on the other side the humble devout, and to some extent the Zealots. But after that date they succeeded so completely in imposing their own view, that this veil still lies not only upon the faces of the Jews, but also upon that of many Christians.

From the point of view of the Christian theologian there is, therefore, no reason why we should not accept in the main the Canon of the Jews. Not for what the scribes intended to give, but for what they actually have handed down, can the Chris-

§ 12. CONCLUSION.

tian church adopt their Canon. In our investigation of the literary treasures of Israel we are concerned to see how its religion, in which Christianity has its roots, originated and maintained itself against all disturbing forces [8]. In the Law and the Prophets the sources for the history of the religion of Israel are opened to us. From them we learn to understand how the testimony of Yahwé through the instrumentality of His prophets made itself known and was able to maintain itself [9]. In the Writings we are permitted to see how far Yahwé's counsel could be fulfilled without the dissolution of the national bond which held Israel's great treasure enclosed; and what influence the testimony of the prophets exerted in Israel [10]. Whatever lies outside these lines is either actually not canonical, or ought not to be [11].

The scribes were not themselves wholly conscious of this *de facto* Canon. The school had to follow; theory came after practise, doctrine after life. And this life, which flourished mostly outside the schools, had often to take a position opposed to them, as Israel's greatest Son opposed His "But I say unto you" to the traditions of the elders [12].

---

[8] From an evolutionist point of view men speak of the development of the religion of Israel. From a different point of

view the history of Israel's religion is called a progressive revelation. We must remember that a progressive revelation from the divine side must evince itself among men as a persistent struggle to master new truths. Every new thought of God is first understood in a soul which has been made receptive for it; and, once grasped, it maintains itself in him who is illumined by it as well as in those around him, only by conflict. This conflict appears to one man as a progressive development; to another, who by experience has learned to know the gulf between God and the human heart as a terrible reality, it appears as a progressive revelation. But however it may be regarded, all are agreed that from the Tora and Nebiim we can understand how the precious treasure of Israel's religion came more and more fully to light and maintained itself ever more firmly.

9 In what chronological order we should arrange the sources, is a question which need not here be discussed at large. All are agreed that the Law and Prophets are almost our only sources for the history of Israel and of its religion. Whether we believe, as tradition would have us, that the prophet Moses (Hosea 12, 1) at once sealed up his prophetic testimony in a written Law; or whether we have come to recognize the testimony of Yahwé through his prophets as an ever-widening stream, in either case the first two divisions of Old Testament Scriptures remain the historical sources for the history of the religion of Israel.

10 To this history belong also the contents of the work of the Chronicler, Chronicles-Ezra-Nehemiah. In it the foundation of the theocracy by Ezra is described, and Chronicles shows us what universal acceptance the priestly views had obtained. Ruth and Lamentations, too, however we take them, contribute to the knowledge of Israel's history down to the establishment of the theocracy. Psalms, Proverbs, and Job show us what influence the prophetic faith in Yahwé exerted in

Israel. The same is true of Ecclesiastes, especially if we sustain the authenticity of the epilogue (Eccl. 12, 9—14). For in that case this book is a proof to us how strongly the belief in Yahwé's righteous retribution had penetrated even into such circles as those in which a book like Koheleth could be written. In the apocalypse of Daniel the believing community expresses its unwavering confidence in the future. (Cf. on notes 9 and 10 and the statements of the text, Buhl, *Kanon u. Text*, p. 72, Engl. transl. p. 72 f., whose conception largely coincides with our own.)

[11] The books of Canticles, and in particular Esther, stand thus properly outside this Canon. If Esther, the object of which is to promote the Festival of Purim, is in so doing maintaining a disguised Feast of the Dead (Schwally, *Leben nach dem Tode*, 1892, p. 42—45), it contains the last spasm of the old naturereligion of Israel, and thus is of itself excluded from the list of books which teach what Yahwé has done in the midst of his people. (Cf. *Letterkunde des O. V.*, § 27, n. 8. 9.) Canticles is a notable production, and not altogether unworthy of its place in the Canon. It is certainly remarkable that we meet in it a protest against polygamy and a warm defence of the love of one man for one woman, albeit in forms which seem to us scarcely decorous. It is then apparent that the prophetic judgment as to the nature of marriage (see Gen 2, 24, and Dillmann's Commentary on this passage), namely, that according to God's intent every man should have his own wife and her only, had found response in Israel, although the religious reason is not brought out. It must be remembered, moreover, that we are not writing an apology for the work of the scribes, but are answering the question why, and how far, the Jewish Canon may be adopted by us. We have no need to grow warm in defence of the *antilegomena* of the Old Testament, about the canonicity of which the Jewish scholars themselves disputed.

Besides, the canonicity of the third collection has certainly always been of a somewhat different character from that of the Law and the Prophets (see § 11, n. 13).

But if Esther, and even Canticles also (unless the allegorical interpretation should help us, see A. Pierson, *Geestelijke Voorouders, I. Israel*, Haarlem, 1887, p. 395, and my *Letterkunde des O. V.*, § 26, n. 4), thus in fact lie outside of the Canon, all the apocrypha are with manifest justice excluded from it; for they contain nothing of value for the history of the establishment of Israel's religion (see W. Robertson Smith, *Old Testament in the Jewish Church*, 2 ed. p. 156). They can scarcely compete in value and importance with any one even of the Kethubim. Jesus Sirach alone might be taken into consideration, but after Proverbs all originality must be denied him. See for the Apocrypha, Dyserinck's Dutch translation, Haarlem, 1874 [in English, *The Variorum Apocrypha*, ed. by C. J. Ball, London: Eyre and Spottiswoode; H. Wace and others: *Commentary on the Apocrypha* ("Speakers Bible"), 1888, 2 vols.], in connection with which it should be noted that in the first century of our era the extent of the Greek Bible was much greater than in later times, so that 4(2) Esdras, Enoch, Ascensio Isaiae, &c., could be accounted part of it. See Schürer, *Geschichte d. Jüd. Volkes*, II. p. 670, ff., *Hist. of the Jewish People, &c.* Div. 2, III. p. 124, ff.

[12] It is because the Jewish scholars did not determine in advance what books should be canonical and what not, and because they were not able to act altogether according to their own views, that we Christians have every reason to be grateful for their precious legacy. Although the life which is of God did not always oppose the schools, it flourished in great part outside of them. Rabbis like Simeon ben Lakish might extol with never so great vehemence the Roll (המגלה), viz. Esther, and even put it on an equality with the Tora, and higher than

Nebiim and Kethubim (§ 6, n. 10), the devout among the people did not seek their edification in it; the Christian church-fathers could not either, and many since their day are equally unable to do so. (Cf. Buhl, *Kanon u. Text*, p. 71, with whose judgment our own in the main agrees.)

But the Jewish scribes were thus, in spite of their defective insight, co-workers in a task the true signifiance of which they themselves did not comprehend. They wove, as it were, upon a costly tapestry, but were placed upon the wrong side, so that they could not see the real pattern. God's way with his children is often thus. But we, who know the true significance of Israel's altogether unique history because we recognize in Jesus Christ the goal toward which all tends, are able to perceive in it all the guiding hand of the great Master-workman.

As long ago as the beginning of the 18th century a learned and pious German theologian, and a champion of orthodoxy, too, wrote these true words: "Canon non uno, quod dicunt, actu ab hominibus, sed paulatim a Deo, animorum temporumque rectore, productus est." (Valentin Loescher, *De causis linguae Ebraeae*, p. 71; see *P. R. E.*[2] VII. p. 424.)

F I N I S.

INDEX OF NAMES AND SUBJECTS.

A.

	Page.
Abarbanel	17.
Abba Ariḥa	60.
Akiba	64 sq , 75, 98, 129, 147, 148.
Alexandria	19, 33, 36, 43.
Alexandrian Canon·	19, 33.
,, Order	45.
Allegorical interpretation (of Canticles)	145.
Alting	130.
Amphilochius	77.
Antilegomena	69, 163.
Apocalypse of Elias	53.
Apocrypha	91 sq.
Apocryphal writings	51 sq., 83, 164.
,, writing of Jeremiah	53.
Apostles	54 sq , 145.
Apostolic Constitutions	79.
Aquila	148.
Armarium Judaicum	93, 140.

	Page.
Arōn	92.
Ascensio Jesaiae	164.
Assumptio Mosis	52.
Athanasius	77.
Augustine	2, 98.
Authority (of the O. T. Canon)	159.
Azariah (de Rossi)	131.

B.

Bacher	123.
Baraitha	60, 61.
Baruch	76, 79.
Bleek	52.
Bloch	4, 66, 88, 90, 130, 135, 137, 149, 150.
Böhl	54, 55.
Bomberg	12.
Bruston	38.
Budde	136.
Buhl	vii, 4, 8, 46, 69, 75, 85, 91, 97, 99, 118, 140, 142, 148, 151, 152.

INDEX OF NAMES AND SUBJECTS.

Burman 130.
Buxtorf 17, 130.

C.

Calvin 138.
Canon 86 sq., 102, 141, 159 sq., &c.
Canticles 51, 62, 72, 139, 142, 144, 145, 163.
Carthage (Council of) 85.
Cheyne 23, 59, 75, 98, 102, 104, 150, 158.
Chronicles (Ezra-Nehemiah) 10, 18, 51, 104, 136 sq., 152, 159, 162, &c.
Chrysostom 25.
Church (Christian) 3, 84, 160.
Closing of the Canon 99, 100, 118, 146, 148, 150.
Collection (of Prophetic Group) 132 sq.
Community 104 sq., 148.
Completion (of the Tora) 109.
Covenant (Book of the) 104.
Cramer 85.
Credner 87.
Crown of the Law 92.
Cyrill of Jerusalem 78.

D.

Dalman (Marx) 59
Daniel 4, 18, 27, 99, 139, 159 &c.
Daubanton 33.

Davidic Psalter 39, 137, 155.
Defiling of hands 88 sq.
Delitzsch 7, 23.
Derenbourg 150.
Deuteronomy 22 sq., 28, 101 sq. 155 &c.
Diestel 2.
Dillmann 23, 163.
Division (of Bibl. books) 11.
„ of Canon 7, 37, 49, 58.
„ into Chapters. 11.
Dodekapropheton 7, 51, 79, 82, 129 &c.
Donum propheticum 17.
Dyserinck 24, 38, 100, 164.
Duhm 23.

E.

Ecclesiastes 51, 64 sq., 74, 84, 99, 139, 143, 149 &c.
Ecclesiastici (libri) 91.
Eichhorn 43.
Eleazar ben Azariah 64, 142.
Elias Levita 2, 57, 72, 124, 129, 131.
Enoch 53, 93, 140, 164.
Epiphanius 53.
Esdras 4 (2) 40 sq., 110, 144, 164.
Essenes 128.
Esther 34, 51, 66, 74, 77 sq., 79, 139, 143, 144, 145, 163, 164 &c.

INDEX OF NAMES AND SUBJECTS. 169

	Page.
Ewald	21, 133.
Exile (Babyl.)	25 sq., 101, 120.
Ezekiel	61, 62, 68 sq., 132 &c.
Ezra	28 sq., 72, 101, 104 sq., 119, 129, 155.
Ezra (Book of), see Chronicles.	

F.

	Page.
Feast of the Law.	9.
,, ,, Dead	163.
Free relation to Canonical Scripture	109 sq.
Frensdorff	135.
Fürst	10, 58, 69, 73, 91, 99, 115, 117, 123, 133, 134, 145, 147, 150, 151, 160.

G.

	Page.
Gamaliel I	68.
Gamaliel II	148, 149.
Ganaz	91 sq.
Geiger	iv, 90, 100, 135, 137, 151.
Gemara	59.
Geniza	92.
Graetz	4, 65, 68, 89, 124, 130, 137, 147, 148 sq., 151.
Gregory Nazianzen	77.
Grotius	53.

H.

	Page.
Hävernick	17.
Haggada	123, 136.
Hagiographa (see also Kethubim)	35, 75, 138 sq., 147, 151.
Halacha	113.
Hananiah ben Hezekiah	68, 73.
Hands (defiling of)	88 sq.
Haphtara	9, 124 sq.
Harduin	55.
Hedging (of the Law)	113.
Hengstenberg	17.
Herzfeld	58.
Hiding away (of books), see ganaz.	
Hierarchy	124, 127.
Hilgenfeld	128.
Hillel (School of)	64.
Hippo (Council of)	85.
Historiography	103 sq.
Hottinger	57.
Hugo de Sto. Caro	11.
Huna b. Ḥiya	67

I.

	Page.
Inspiration	16, 66.
Isaiah	133 &c.

J.

	Page.
Jacob ben Ḥayim	11.
Jeremiah	133 &c.
Jerome	2, 14, 20, 25 &c.
Jesus	54 sq., 145, 153, 160, 165.
Job	61, 139, 153, 155 sq.
Johanan ben Joshua	64.

INDEX OF NAMES AND SUBJECTS.

	Page.
Johanan ben Zakkai	89.
Jonah	63 sq., 112 &c.
Jonathan (Rabbi)	66.
de Jong	32, 149.
Jose	64.
Josephus (Flavius)	19, 42 sq., 127, 146.
Joshua	104, 111 &c.
Josiah	22, 101 sq.
Jost	65.
Judah (Rabbi, ben Ilai)	64, 67, 142.
Judah b. Ezekiel	60.
Judah I (ha-Kadosh)	60, 142.
Judas (Maccabaeus)	40.
Judges	18, 25, 117 &c.

K.

Kabbala	71, 96 sq., 160.
Kabisch	41.
Keil	17, 23, 91.
Kethubim	117, 138, 140 sq., 144, 160 &c.
„ Aharonim	10, 143, 147 sq. &c.
„ Rishonim	10, 147 sq. &c.
Kimhi	3, 17, 57, 70.
Kihn	85.
Kings	18, 25, 103, 117 &c.
Kithbe hakkodesh	5, 151.
König	23, 28, 29, 58, 69.

	Page.
Kosters	100
Krochmal	149.
Kuenen	i, 13, 16, 22, 30, 37, 45, 55, 83, 102, 106, 107, 108, 109, 110, 126, 130, 135, 139, 141, 149, 150, 151.

L.

Lamentations	10, 11, 19, 83, 139 sq. &c.
Langton, Stephen	12.
Laodicea (Council of)	77.
Law	5, 29, 36, 93 sq., 97 sq., 101 sq., 104 sq., 111 sq., 144, 155 sq., 160, 161.
„ of Holiness	107.
„ oral	69, 96, 111 sq.
Levi b. Samuel	67.
Levitical Psalter.	151.
Loescher	165.

M.

1 Maccabees	91, 94 sq., 100.
2 „	91, 100.
Maccabean Psalms	138.
Maimonides	16.
Martyrium Jesaiae	52.
Marti	159.
Marx (Dalman)	13, 15, 59, 60, 61.
Megilloth (public reading of)	14.
Meïr	142, 147.

	Page.
Melito of Sardis	76 sq.
Midrash	122.
Mishna	59, 146 sq.
Mosaic	156.
Müller, Joel	15.
Munus propheticum	17.

N.

Names (of the Holy Scriptures) 5 sq., 47.
Nebiim 7, 114 sq., 142, 155 sq., 160 sq. &c.
„ Aharonim 7, 119, 123, 133.
„ Rishonim 7, 117, 123.
Nehemiah 28, 37, 105 sq., 115, 119, 137, 139.
„ (Book of), see Chronicles.
Nestle 12.
Nestorian Canon. 85.
Neubauer 59.
Nöldeke 85, 92, 147.
Noordtzij 54.
Number (of O. T. books) 10, 40, 41, 42, 76, 80, 146.

O.

Oehler 18, 21.
Oort 4, 50, 110, 112, 136, 145, 147, 148, 158.
Oral law, see Law.

	Page.
Order (of O. T. books)	7, 11, 45, 141, 151 sq.
v. Orelli	123.
Origen	2, 53, 76 sq., 88, 100, 127.

P.

Parasha 8.
Paul 3, 158, 159.
People (of the Book) 106, 110.
People's Bible 55.
„ Book 104, 108.
Peshito 85.
Pharisees 126.
Philo (Alexandrinus) 35, 36 sq.
Pierson 164.
Pick, B. 36.
Popper 110.
Priests 26, 126 sq.
Priestly Law 28 sq., 104 sq., 109.
Prophetic historians 45.
Prophecy (Cessation of) 112, 119, 120, 122, 123.
Proverbs 62 sq., 74, 139, 156 sq. &c.
Psalms 24, 49, 137, 144, 155 sq. &c.
Pseudepigraphic writings 122.
Public reading of Scripture 8, 9, 14, 92, 121, 145.

R.

Rabbi, see Abba Ariha.
Rashi 61, 67.

… INDEX OF NAMES AND SUBJECTS.

	Page.
Rashi (Pseudo)	63, 71.
Rau	130.
Reading (public) in synagogue, see Public reading.	
Redaction (of Hexateuch)	108 sq., 134 sq.
„ (of Nebiim)	119 sq., 134.
„ (of Kethubim)	147 sq.
Resch	53.
Reuss	108.
Riehm	49.
Rutgers	32.
Ruth	10, 19, 83, 112, 139 &c.
Ryle	vii, 4, 53.

S.

	Page.
Sadducees	126 sq.
Sadducean Canon	127 sq.
Samaritans	106, 110 sq.
Samuel (Book of)	18, 25, 103 &c.
Samuel (Rabbi)	66, 88, 150.
Samuel (ben Nachman)	66.
Schiffer	65.
Schiller-Szinessy	12.
Schürer	4, 38, 53, 55, 100, 114, 129, 164.
Schwab	66, 73.
Schwally	163.
Scribes	125 sq., 156 sq. &c.
Semler	87.
Sepharim	27, 116, 139.

	Page.
Sepher Hayyashar	24.
„ Milḥamoth Jahwé	24.
Sepp	48.
Septuagint	12, 19, 33 sq.
Simeon ben Azzai	64.
Simeon ben Lakish	75, 164.
Simeon ben Manasseh	64.
Sirach, Jesus ben	30 sq., 91, 94 sq., 98, 118, 133.
Sirach (grandson of)	32 sq., 116, 118, 138.
Shammai, School of	64, 149
Shelomo ben Ishmael	12.
Smend	121.
Smith, W. Robertson	4, 77, 92, 95, 121, 122, 132, 134, 148, 164.
Song of Songs (of Solomon), see Canticles.	
Standard (see also Touchstone)	2, 3, 25, 43, 93 sq.
Stekhoven, Schuurmans	34.
Stier	51.
Strack [art. Kanon in P. R. E.[2] &c.]	1, 3, 4, 6, 9, 12, 59, 74, 92, 98, 114, 123.
Surenhusius	51, 58.
Synagogue (The Great)	16, 62, 73, 125 sq., 129 sq., 135, 147.

T.

Teba	92, 140.

INDEX OF NAMES AND SUBJECTS.

	Page.
Tertullian	6, 93, 127, 140.
Testament (New)	47 sq.
,, (Old)	6, 22 sq.
Text (of the O. T.)	109, 135, 136.
Tikkunē Sopherim	135 sq.
Theocracy	119 sq., 124.
Theodore (of Mopsuestia)	85.
Tora, see Law.	
Tora and Sepharim.	140.
Tora-feast, see Feast of the Law.	
Touchstone	93 sq.
Tradition (as to Canon of O. T.)	2, 16, 54, 57, 125, 153 &c.
,, Prophets, of the Law	71, 96.
Trent (Council of)	2.

V.

Valeton Jr.	134.
Valeton Sr.	157.
Vernes.	102.
Vitringa	130.

W.

Weber	89, 90, 94, 97, 98.
Wellhausen	24, 80, 86, 92, 101, 126, 131, 150.
de Wette-Schrader	11, 12, 76, 78, 79, 80, 85.
Wisdom of Solomon	75, 91 &c.
Witsius	17, 130.
Wildeboer (Letterkunde, &c.)	viii, 29, 54, 62, 102, 106, 134, 138, 143, 150, 157, 163, 164.
Wünsche	65, 70, 142.

Z.

Zahn	7.
Zealots	160.
Zunz	9, 63, 96, 107.

INDEX OF PASSAGES FROM BIBLE, TALMUD &c.

Reference	Page.	Reference	Page.
Gen. 1, 1—6, 9	9.	Num. 2, 8	157.
Gen. 2, 24	163.	Num. 4, 35	112.
Gen. 6, 9—Ch. 11, 32	9.	Num. 8, 23—26	112.
Gen. 36, 33	61.	Num. 12, 8	16.
Gen. 47, 28	8.	Num. 21, 14	24.
Ex. 17, 14	67.	Num. 22, 2—25, 9	61.
Ex. 20, 23—23, 33	104.	Num. 28, 1—9	109.
Ex. 25, 22	23.	Deut. 7, 3	109.
Ex. 29, 38—42	30, 109.	Deut. 14, 1 ff.	26.
Ex. 30, 11—16	30, 109.	Deut. 16, 13—15	108.
Ex. 31, 18	23.	Deut. 17, 18	103.
Ex. 35—40	109 f.	Deut. 18, 18	122.
Ex. 38, 21	23.	Deut. 23, 3—5	29.
Ex. 40, 20	23.	Deut. 24, 8	26, 103.
Lev. 1—7	26.	Deut. 28, 49	49.
Lev. 17—26	26, 107.	Deut. 30, 12	96.
Lev. 18, 25, 27	109.	Deut. 31, 9	23, 103.
Lev. 23, 39	108.	Deut. 31, 19	24.
Lev. 24, 3	23.	Deut. 31, 26	23.
Lev. 27, 32, 33	30, 109.	Deut. 34, 5	61.
Lev. 27, 34	67.	Jos. 8, 34	140.
Num. 1, 21, 23	79.	Jos. 10, 13	24, 140.

INDEX OF PASSAGES FROM BIBLE, TALMUD &C.

	Page.		Page.
Jos. 24, 25	23.	Jer. 1, 8, 17	27.
Jos. 24, 26	23.	Jer. 1, 9	121.
1 Sam. 9, 9	18.	Jer. 5, 3	27.
1 Sam. 10, 25	23.	Jer. 11	104.
2 Sam. 1, 10	24.	Jer. 19, 15	55.
2 Sam. 1, 18	24.	Jer. 23, 9—40	121.
2 Kings 1, 3	122.	Jer. 25	121.
2 Kings 11, 12	24.	Jer. 25, 11, 12	29.
2 Kings 22, 23	102.	Jer. 25, 13	134.
2 Kings 23, 2 ff.	22.	Jer. 26, 23	49.
Is. 1—39	133, 134.	Jer. 27	134.
Is. 3, 1	27.	Jer. 29	121.
Is. 3, 3	70.	Jer. 29, 10	29.
Is. 4, 3	102.	Jer. 31, 29 ff.	121.
Is. 6.	134.	Jer. 46—51	134.
Is. 6, 13	102.	Jer. 52	133.
Is. 8, 2	50.	Ezekiel 2, 8 ff.	121.
Is. 8, 16	120.	Ezek. 3, 9	27.
Is. 11, 1—9	102.	Ezek. 4, 16	27.
Is. 20	134.	Ezek. 13	121.
Is. 25, 8	128.	Ezek. 14, 14	99, 143.
Is. 26, 19	128.	Ezek. 20 & 28, 3	99.
Is. 28	134.	Ezek. 18, 2	121.
Is. 28, 11	48.	Ezek. 40—48	26, 67, 106.
Is. 34, 15, 16	22 f.	Ezek. 44, 5—28	113.
Is. 40—66	133.	Hos. 1, 2	13.
Is. 42, 5—43, 11.	9.	Hos. 12, 1	162.
Is. 45, 19—21	27.	Joel 2, 13	71.
Is. 46, 8—13	121.	Amos 4, 11	29.
Is. 54, 1—10	9.	Amos 7, 12 ff.	18.
Is. 55, 3	117.	Jonah 3, 10	71.
Is. 56, 1—8	158.	Hab. 2, 20	29.

INDEX OF PASSAGES FROM BIBLE, TALMUD &c.

	Page.		Page.
Zech. 1, 1	50.	Ezra 3, 2, 3	28.
Zech. 1, 12	29.	Ezra 5, 1	50.
Zech. 2, 17	29.	Ezra 6, 12	126.
Zech. 3, 2	29.	Ezra 6, 16	28.
Zech. 9—14	133.	Ezra 7, 6	105.
Zech. 9, 1	133.	Ezra 7, 14, 25	26, 105.
Zech. 11, 12	52.	Ezra 8, 15 ff.	113.
Zech. 12, 1	133.	Ezra 9 & 19	28.
Zech. 13, 3	122.	Ezra 9, 11	109, 122, 157.
Mal. 1, 1	133.	Ezra 10	29.
Mal. 4, 5, 6	122.	Ezra 10, 3	104.
Ps. 3—41	40, 138.	Ezra 10, 11	126.
Ps. 40, 8	24.	Neh. 8—10	26, 105, 110, 115, 131.
Ps. 72, 20	138.		
Ps. 78, 1	160.	Neh. 8, 8	5.
Ps. 79, 2	138.	Neh. 8, 10	29, 106, 107, 125.
Ps. 83	138.	Neh. 8, 18.	108.
Ps. 84, 5	98.	Neh. 9, 2	126.
Prov. 25, 1	24, 39.	Neh. 9, 3	108.
Cant. 6, 8	70.	Neh. 10, 4, 10	131.
Ruth 4, 18—22	10.	Neh. 10, 9	131.
Eccl. 1, 3	65.	Neh. 10, 29	108, 126.
Eccl. 1, 13	96.	Neh. 10, 30—39	108.
Eccl. 12, 9—14	149, 163.	Neh. 10, 33	109.
Eccl. 12, 13, 14	65.	Neh. 10, 34	109.
Esther 9, 31	77.	Neh. 10, 38—40	109.
Dan. 9, 2	27, 116, 117, 140.	Neh. 12, 44—47	109.
Dan. 9, 10	160.	Neh. 13, 5, 12	109.
Dan. 12, 2, 3	128.	Neh. 13, 28	110, 112.
Ezra 1—6	28.	1 Chron. 23, 24—27	113.
Ezra 1, 1 f.	142.	1 Chron. 29, 29	140.
Ezra 2	28.	2 Chron. 24, 20, 21	50.

INDEX OF PASSAGES FROM BIBLE, TALMUD &C.

	Page.		Page.
2 Chron. 24, 27.	143.	Acts. 9, 2	114.
2 Chron. 36, 23.	142.	Acts. 13, 15	9, 48
		Acts. 13, 17	9.
		Acts. 18, 24	48.
Matt. 5, 17	48.	Acts. 19, 9, 23.	114.
Matt. 6, 5	95.	Acts. 24, 22	114.
Matt. 7, 12	48.	Acts. 28, 23	48.
Matt. 7, 29	154.	Jas. 1, 9	52.
Matt. 15, 2	114.	Jas. 4, 5	53.
Matt. 22, 23—32	128.	1 Pet. 1, 6, 7	52.
Matt. 22, 29	48.	2 Pet. 1, 20	48.
Matt. 22, 31 f.	127.	Jude vs. 9, 14—26	52, 53.
Matt. 22, 40	48.	Rom. 1, 2	48.
Matt. 23, 2, 3	56, 145.	Rom. 1, 20—32	52.
Matt. 23, 35	14, 47, 49, 50.	Rom. 5, 20	158.
Matt. 24, 15	18.	Rom. 11, 2	10.
Matt. 27, 9	52, 54, 55.	1 Cor. 2, 9	52, 53.
Mark. 2, 26	10.	1 Cor. 6, 13	52.
Mark. 7, 3	114.	1 Cor. 14, 21	6, 48, 98.
Mark. 12, 26	10.	2 Cor. 3, 14	5.
Luk. 4, 16, 17	9.	Gal. 3, 17	6.
Luk. 11, 49	52, 53, 54.	Eph. 5, 14	52, 53.
Luk. 11, 51	49, 50.	2 Tim. 3, 8	52.
Luk. 16, 16, 29, 31	48.	2 Tim. 3, 15	48.
Luk. 24, 26, 27	49.	Heb. 1, 3	52.
Luk. 24, 44	47, 49, 158.	Heb. 9, 15—17	6.
Joh. 7, 38	52, 53.	Heb. 11, 34, 35	52.
Joh. 10, 34	6, 48, 98.	Heb. 11, 37	52.
Joh. 10, 35	48.		
Joh. 12, 34	6, 48, 98.		
Joh. 15, 25	6.	1 Macc. 4, 46	122.
Joh. 19, 36	48.	1 Macc. 7, 16, 17	138.

INDEX OF PASSAGES FROM BIBLE, TALMUD &C.

Reference	Page.
1 Mac. 7, 48	77.
1 Mac. 9, 27	122.
2 Macc. 1, 1—9 & 1, 10—2, 18	38.
2 Macc. 2, 13, 36 ff.	115, 119, 137.
2 Macc. 2, 14	40.
2 Macc. 6, 18—7, 42	52.
Wisd. of Sol. 3, 3—7	52.
Wisd. of Sol. 7, 26	52.
Wisd. of Sol. 13—15	52.
Jes. Sir. 2, 16.	31.
Jes. Sir. 4, 29	52.
Jes. Sir. 5, 11	52.
Jes. Sir. 15, 1—8	31.
Jes. Sir. 19, 20—24	31.
Jes. Sir. 24, 22; 23, 33	31, 94.
Jes. Sir. 25, 7—11	31.
Jes. Sir. 35, 14—16.	31.
Jes. Sir. 35, 23—36, 3	31.
Jes. Sir. 36, 20	52.
Jes. Sir. 39, 1 ff.	31.
Jes. Sir. 44—49	31.
Jes. Sir. 48, 22—25	133.
Jes. Sir. 49, 14—16	31.
3 (1) Esdras 3, 12	v.
3 (1) Esdras 4, 41	v.
4 (2) Esdras 5, 24, 26	145.
4 (2) Esdras 7, 26	145.
4 (2) Esdras 14, 18—47.	40.

Reference	Page.
Pea ii, 6	114.
Taanith ii, 1	71.
Megilla iii, 1	140.
Megilla 7a	63, 88, 89.
Sanhedrin x, 1 fol. 28a	99.
Eduyoth v, 3	63, 65, 89, 149.
Eduyoth viii, 7	114.
Aboth i, 1	97, 113, 114, 129.
Aboth i, 2	130, 131.
Kelim xv, 6	90, 91.
Yadaïm iii, 5	63, 64, 89.
Yadaïm iii, 6	89.
Yadaïm iv, 3	114.
Yadaïm iv, 6	89.
Shabbath 116b	93.
Shabbath 13b	63, 68.
Shabbath 30b	63, 65.
Shabbath 14a	89, 90.
Shabbath 30ab	63, 84.
Taanith 9a	97.
Taanith 15a	63, 71, 74.
Megilla 7a	65, 66.
Moed Katan 5a	69.
Hagiga 13a	63, 68.
Baba bathra 13b	141.
Baba bathra 14b	133.
Baba bathra 14b, 15a	13, 83.
Baba bathra 15a	125, 129.
Baba bathra 15	73.
Sanhedrin 21b	73.
Sanhedrin x. 1, fol. 28a	99.
Sanhedrin 91b	5, 98.

INDEX OF PASSAGES FROM BIBLE, TALMUD &C.

	Page.		Page.
Sanhedrin 99a	95.	Aboth de R. Nathan, c. i	
Sanhedrin 100a	63, 67.		63, 150.
Sanhedrin 100b	99.	Mechilta 64b	96.
Menahoth 30a	61.	Leviticus Rabba, sec. 28	63, 65.
Menahoth 45a	63, 67.	Numeri Rabba, sec. 18	63, 70.
Jesus Megilla i, 8 (11) fol.		Numeri Rabba 10	97.
71b	73.	Deut. Rabba 8	96.
Jesus Megilla i, 4 (fol. 70d)		Ruth Rabba 32a	97.
	63, 66, 129.	Midrash Koheleth 1, 3	63.
Jesus Megilla iii, 1 (fol. 73d)		Midrash Koheleth 63d	96.
	142.	Midrash Koheleth 1, 3	65.
Sanhedrin x, 1	95.	Tanchuma Re'eh 1	160.
Sopherim iii, 1 p. v.	15, 142.	Tanchuma 26a	135.
Sopherim iii, 6	14.	Moré Nebochim ii, 45	16.
Sopherim iii, 9	92.		

ERRATA.

Page 6, l. 4, *for* Yawhé *read* Yahwé.
p. 7, l. 2, *read* נביאים.
p. 8, l. 2, *read* פרשה.
p. 8. l. 7, *read* פתוחה.
p. 10, l. 11, *read* כתובים גדולים.
p. 22, l. 15, *omit the comma after* pre-exilic.
p. 26, l. 3, *for* was *read* were.
p. 28, l. 15, *omit* to.
p. 29, l. 14, *omit* to *before* belong.
p. 34, l. 16, *insert a comma after* son.
p. 37, l. 25, *read* ’αναθεμάτων.
p. 44, l. 1, *read* ὀλίγῳ.
p. 50, l. 29, *for* Zach. *read* Zech.
p. 53, l. 6, *for* Jac. *read* Jas.
p. 57, l. 18, *read* ’αναμφισβήτητον.
p. 60, l. 1, *read* filiis.
p. 61, l. 21, *read* subscription.
p. 64, l. 20, *put a colon in the place of the period.*
p. 65, l. 8, *for* consist *read* consists.
p. 74, l. 18, *insert* the *before* greater part.
p. 76, note, *read* supports.
  „   „   *read* ’Αριθμοί.
p. 78, l. 18, *read* θεόκλητος.

ERRATA.

Page 80, l. 26, *read* instaurationem.
  p. 82, l. 11, *read* significantius.
  p. 86, l. 19, *insert* was *before* not.
  p. 89, l. 5, *read* הספר.
  p. 93, l. 2, *read* silently.
  „ „ l. 22, *read* significance.
  p. 95, l. 30, *read* canonical.
  p. 96, l. 18, *read* observed.
  „ „ l. 19, *read* has.
  p. 98, l. 14, *for* come *read* came.
  p. 101, l. 15, *read* assuming.
  p. 106, l. 11, *for* absolute *read* absolutely.
  p. 108, l. 3, *read* fulfilling.
  p. 109, l. 20, *read* pre-priestly.
  p. 113, l. 18, *omit the point at the end of the line.*
  p. 117, l. 30, *read* collection.
  p. 123, l. 22, *for* became *read* become.
  p. 125, l. 12, *for* works *read* work.
  „ l. 18, *insert* the *before* sacred.
  p. 128, l. 19, *read* remarks.
  p. 135, l. 29, *read* teach.
  p. 140, l. 12, *omit the comma at the end of the line.*
  „ last line, *read* admittitur.
  p. 143, l. 29, *for* of *read* to.
  p. 144, l. 23, *for* there *read* these.
  p. 154, l. 3, *insert* in *after* lived.
  p. 158, l. 13, *read* Israel.
  p. 159, l. 4, *read* explained.

www.ingramcontent.com/pod-product-compliance
Lightning Source LLC
Chambersburg PA
CBHW071423160426
43195CB00013B/1790